Nature of Belief

A textbook for Intermediate 1 and 2
Scottish Qualifications Authority
National Qualifications in

Religious, Moral and Philosophical Studies

Joe Walker

Hodder Gibson

A MEMBER OF THE HODDER HEADLINE GROUP

Photo Acknowledgements

The publishers would like to thank the following individuals, institutions and companies for permission to reproduce photographs in this book. Every effort has been made to trace ownership of copyright. The publishers would be happy to make arrangements with any copyright holder whom it has not been possible to contact:

Bruce Design Limited (34 bottom), British Film Institute (201), Cafod (166), Christian Aid (165), Corbis (5, 14, 46, 47, 53, 54, 56, 83, 98, 148, 152, 154, 179 both, 190, 196, 199, 200, 209, 211), Imperial War Museum (59), Novosti (151, 195), PA Photos (53, 54), Ronald Grant archive (3, 41), Science Photo Library (16, 24, 34, 106, 125, 127).

Orders: please contact Bookpoint Ltd, 130 Milton Park, Abingdon, Oxon OX14 4SB. Telephone: (44) 01235 827720. Fax: (44) 01235 400454. Lines are open from 9.00 – 6.00, Monday to Saturday, with a 24 hour message answering services. You can also order through our website. www.hoddereducation.co.uk

Note about the Internet links in the book. The user should be aware that URLs or web addresses change regularly. Every effort has been made to ensure the accuracy of the URLs provided in this book on going to press. It is inevitable, however, that some will change. It is sometimes possible to find a relocated web page by just typing in the address of the home page for a website in the URL window of your browser.

British Library Cataloguing in Publication Data
A catalogue record for this title is available from the British Library

ISBN-10: 0 340 87237 3
ISBN-13: 978 0 340 87237 6

Published by Hodder Gibson, 2a Christie Street, Paisley PA1 1NB.
Tel: 0141 848 1609; Fax: 0141 889 6315; email: hoddergibson@hodder.co.uk
First published 2003
Impression number 10 9 8 7 6 5 4 3
Year   2008 2007 2006 2005

Papers used in this book are natural, renewable and recyclable products. They are made from wood grown in sustainable forests. The logging and manufacturing processes conform to the environmental regulations of the country of origin.

Typeset by Fakenham Photosetting Limited, Fakenham, Norfolk
Printed by Arrowsmith, Bristol for Hodder Gibson, 2a Christie Street, Paisley, PA1 1NB, Scotland, UK

Acknowledgements

The author would like to thank the following: Lorna and David, as ever, for their patience and understanding while I was yet again chained to the computer (or amending soggy drafts when I should have been cheering on Livingston Aquanauts at another gala). Tony Dane, for being without a poolside assistant on Tuesdays... beyond November!

Thanks to Patricia Stevenson, SQA Principal Assessor for Intermediate 1 and 2, for comments on the proposal and early drafts. Thanks also to pupils at Liberton High School who have had the materials tried out on them in various forms as they have been developed.

Thanks also to those at Hodder & Stoughton – and now Hodder Gibson in Scotland who have been very patient and supportive during my various projects. Especially to Lis Tribe, John Mitchell – the grand fromage of Hodder Gibson, Katherine Bennett, the desk editor who worked through the MS and Moira Munro whose illustrations have brought the text to life.

About the Author

Joe Walker is Head of Religious, Moral and Philosophical Studies at Liberton High School in Edinburgh. He was Secretary of ATRES for four years. He was part of the original Central Support Group during the development of Standard Grade Religious Studies, has marked Standard Grade since its inception, and now also marks Intermediate 1 and 2 papers.

He was, for four years, a member of the Scottish Examination Board, and then Scottish Qualifications Authority, Religious Studies Panel. As part of this work he has been responsible for vetting, setting, moderating and many other tasks for the SQA. He is the writer of a range of support materials and NAB items for the HSDU, then SQA, at all levels, including Advanced Higher Bioethics. He was Development Officer for RME for the City of Edinburgh Council.

This is his first textbook with Hodder Gibson. However, his other titles with Hodder & Stoughton are; *Our World: Religion and Environment* (0340 605499); *Their World: Religion and Animal Issues* (0340 721162); *World Issues: Religion and Morality* (with Jim Green) (0340 781815); *Environmental Ethics* (0340 757701); *Making Moral Decisions* (0340 802030); *Making Moral Decisions – Support Edition* (0340 846275); *Connections Series; Books A, B and C* (including Foundation Editions) (with Libby Ahluwalia; Ann Lovelace; Jon Mayled and Joy White) (0340 804 84X; 0340 804866; 0340 804882).

To the Teacher

This textbook supports the delivery of SQA National Qualifications at Intermediate 1 and 2 in Religious Moral and Philosophical Studies. The material may be used with certificate classes, but is also suitable for use with non-certificate S3 and S4 pupils – or those who will follow the Nature of Belief Unit as a stand-alone unit. Teachers should satisfy themselves that they are working from the most recent SQA arrangements documents, and that they understand the methods of assessment employed in the National Qualifications Programme, *including any changes subsequent to the National Qualifications Review.* The text is not designed as a distance learning scheme.

The aim is to provide, where possible, a lighter touch, given the weighty nature of many of the issues in the course. Hopefully, without trivialising the issues themselves.

I'd welcome comments, advice or suggestions for any subsequent publications or revisions to this one, as well as any comments which arise from the use of this book. Feel free to allow your pupils to contact me with their views.

Contact: mobyjoe1uk@yahoo.co.uk

Contents

The Nature Of Belief

You're sitting in the school canteen. In walks the new RE teacher. Delicately balanced on his head are a tomato and a carrot. Other teachers greet him normally. Someone pulls up a chair for him, beckoning him to join them at their table. Other pupils nod to him and say "Hiya Sir". It would seem only you notice the carrot and the tomato. He drops his fork. As he bends down to retrieve it his tomato falls to the floor. One of the science teachers picks it up and places it back onto your RE teacher's head. He gets stuck into his lunch, and they all start chatting about teacher things . . .

Is this normal?

We all have beliefs

Unless your own life is full of oddness, you're probably wondering why this RE teacher has a carrot and a tomato on his head. Why's he doing it? Is he normal? Whatever you think of it, it'll get you questioning, examining and reflecting.

Beliefs are about the ways in which we try to make sense of things. What you believe is your attempt to understand

> **Task**
> What would you do in such a situation, and why would you do it?

1

everything and the part you play in it all. This course aims to get you thinking about the beliefs we have. Some beliefs are fairly ordinary – like believing that one brand of cornflakes is better than another. Others are more serious – like believing that you will be rewarded for all eternity for some act which most others would consider to be wrong.

Beliefs have real power. They can influence people's lives for good or bad. People live by their beliefs. People die for their beliefs. No matter what you believe, you believe something. Even if you believe nothing! You live your life constantly testing out your beliefs.

Imagine you get on the bus today, and before you allow the driver to move off you demand to see his driving licence, breathalyse him and quiz him on the highway code. You might find you get some funny looks from your fellow passengers ... some might even get off a stop or two early. This doesn't happen because you just believe that the driver is properly qualified to do his job.

This is a belief you can confirm every day by your own experience. But there are other kinds too. Ask around in your class:

◆ Who believes in ghosts?

◆ Who believes in life on other planets?

◆ Who believes the earth is round?

◆ Who believes they'll wake up tomorrow?

◆ Who believes in God?

◆ Who believes in miracles?

And so on.

No matter what answer they give to these kinds of questions, their answers show what they believe. Even a "not sure" answer is a statement of belief. Planning your life based on the idea that you'll wake up tomorrow morning is also an act of belief. See, we all have beliefs.

Where do beliefs come from?

The obvious answer is that beliefs come from many sources.

◆ From your upbringing

◆ Your own experience

◆ Other people's experience

Task
Prepare a graffiti wall in your classroom. In the centre write "I Believe". Around this, people should be able to anonymously write a sentence or two.

◆ Your working things out

◆ The teachings of people who know more than you

◆ You sometimes maybe even believe just what you want to believe.

Why bother?

Looking at the possible consequences of your beliefs is one of the most important things you will ever do in your entire life, because beliefs can make the world a safer or more dangerous place. Just accepting things, without thinking them through at least a bit can be a pretty scary thing to do.

Imagine someone offers you a food you've never eaten before. It looks like a cross between trifle and Spaghetti Bolognese. They won't tell you what's in it, all they say is "eat it, it's good for you". Most sensible people would ask a few questions about it, and treat this new food with a bit of care. They'll probably ask the other person to eat a bit first, but then, Snow White did that and look where it got her. Maybe it'll kill you, maybe it'll turn you into a raving madman who'll run around setting people's sporrans on fire . . .

Watch what you eat?

It's amazing how many people will allow their beliefs to lead them into doing things which are quite odd or dangerous. Many teenagers don't really think through what they believe – they just accept things because their parents believe it, or their friends do, or it's fashionable to . . . And these are people who don't really like to be told what to do!

Thinking about what we do is one of the major things which makes us different from any other living thing on planet earth. Of course, we could just not bother. But what kind of world would that be? Imagine the surgeon who simply says I can't be bothered thinking about this operation, I'm away home, it's too much work. Or if he said to himself in the middle of an operation ... this is pointless, I don't believe that this person deserves to live, so I'll just make a wee accidental cut here ...

Beliefs can give meaning to life, or make life seem meaningless. They can be used to take advantage of people, or they can be used to give people power. People can be chained to their beliefs, or their beliefs can set them free.

Proof

Many people today don't believe what they can't prove. Then they continue to live their lives as normal, expecting that they'll still be around next week, which, of course, they can't prove. If you asked people in your class about their beliefs about God, you'd probably find a lot of them said "There's no proof". But they might be the same people who need no proof that their parents love them. Maybe not everything's provable, but then again, maybe it is – it depends on your belief.

Beliefs: good, bad and ugly

A man walks onto a bus. The bus is full of schoolchildren. He looks around at the smiling kids, messing about as usual in anticipation of another day at school. A quiet one in the corner reading. Two girls talking, between their giggles, about a boy at the front of the bus. A younger one pleading with his older sister to help him finish the homework he should have done for today.

It's a hot spring day, but he's wearing a heavy winter coat. He looks like he must be fairly overweight beneath the coat. Sadly, it's not just a fat man. The bombs strapped to his body give him an inhuman bulk. The man is happy. Soon he will be exactly where he wants to be. He believes that he'll be rewarded for his good life. He smiles at a child. He reaches inside his coat. It is only a matter of connecting two tiny wires with the turn of a switch ...

Task

Discuss: What things do you believe in without needing proof? Can everything be proved? Does it matter whether there's proof for your beliefs or not?

Task

Discuss: How often do you think or talk about what you believe? What kind of beliefs do you have? Should your beliefs be private? How can beliefs affect life? Do beliefs ever change?

Beliefs can lead to tragedy

Sometimes people's beliefs lead them to acts of violence or cruelty. At the same time, these people may truly believe that what they are doing is right. Sometimes beliefs lead to people doing great things. For example, Martin Luther King, Mother Teresa and Mahatma Gandhi are all people whose beliefs have led them to change the world – or at least challenge it. They lived by their beliefs and some of them died for them.

Beliefs have great power to change the way you are – and once you have changed yourself, then you can change the world. People don't have to be world famous to make a difference. Every day people all over the world do kind and selfless things because they believe it's right to do so.

> **Task**
>
> Discuss: How much do you think your beliefs affect your daily life? Give some examples.

Reflection

The philosopher Plato said,

"The unexamined life is not worth living"

He meant that examining our beliefs is what makes us truly human. This means putting our beliefs to the test, but also questioning them. It's not just about learning more facts and opinions. It's about working out how we feel about the issues and ideas involved – because this can help us to get a better picture of who we are and how we fit into this very complicated world. We can't reject what we haven't tried to understand. We should also be careful about accepting something which we don't understand.

Imagine you walked into your RMPS class for the first ever lesson. Your new teacher – who has never taught you –

screams "Out of my room, I'm not teaching you!". You'd be quite justified in thinking that this teacher had lost the plot. Your response would probably be instant – "Why is this teacher treating me like this when he doesn't even know me?". And yet, very often in life that's just what we do with beliefs and ideas. We make up our minds before we've taken the time to really find out about it and think it through.

Thinking it through is what this course is all about.

Task

Discuss: How many times have you said "I've never really thought about it"? What kinds of things have you said this about?

The technical bits

There are three sections to this National Qualification in RMPS.

◆ The Existence of God

◆ Science and Belief

◆ Belief and Action

You study only one. But you'll find that there's sometimes overlap between the different sections. In each section there are smaller parts. You study them all, and you'll be assessed in more than one, but you'll only answer on one section in the final exam. You'll have an assignment to do too, which the information in this book should help you with.

Of course, you might just be following this unit in your RMPS class alone, and might have only Unit Assessments to do. If so, enjoy.

RMPS means:

◆ **Religion**: How have people around the world (and through time) tried to understand the meaning and purpose of life, and developed sets of ideas about what is true and what isn't?

◆ **Morality**: How have people responded to the issues we all face in life? How have they decided what's right and wrong?

◆ **Philosophy**: How have people tried to answer life's big questions? How helpful have these answers been? How true are they?

The *outcomes* of your studies are:

◆ You should be able to show that you understand what issues of belief are

◆ You should be able to analyse beliefs – take them apart and work out what you think of them

◆ You should be able to evaluate beliefs –you should be able to weigh up different views about beliefs and come to your own conclusions.

In the real world, this means you should be able to:

◆ Describe issues of belief

◆ Explain why the issue might be a challenge for religious people

◆ Explain how religious people might respond to this challenge

◆ Express you own opinion on issues of belief (and also be able to explain different viewpoints at Intermediate 2)

◆ Support your own opinion with reasonable argument.

BIG WARNING

REMEMBER, THIS BOOK (AND THIS COURSE) IS **NOT** TRYING TO TEACH YOU WHAT YOU SHOULD BELIEVE.

IT IS TRYING TO TEACH YOU TO **THINK** ABOUT WHAT YOU BELIEVE, AND WHAT OTHERS BELIEVE.

THERE ARE NO EASY ANSWERS IN THIS COURSE, BUT THERE ARE LOTS OF INTERESTING QUESTIONS.

ALL YOU ARE ASKED TO DO IS THINK.

Activities

1 Do you think it is important to think about beliefs? Explain your reasons for your answer.

2 Does it really matter what anyone believes?

3 If you can't prove something, does it make any sense to believe it?

4 When do you think people are most likely to ask questions about belief? Why do you think this is so?

5 How can beliefs lead to good things?

6 How can beliefs be dangerous?

7 How can beliefs help make sense of life?

8 Do you agree that the unexamined life is not worth living?

The Argument from Design

Rab and Donnie

Proposing the design argument

Rab and Donnie are at the football. Their team's not doing so well this season. It's half-time and they're 2–0 down ... again. Over Bovril and a pie, Rab's been looking at the fanzine. He turns to Donnie and in a cynical tone says ...

RAB: Whit's this all aboot then?

DONNIE: Aye, pretty dire, eh. Ah blame the defence.

RAB: Naw, ya eejit. This [he points to the fanzine], oor star striker's only found Jesus. Whit d'ye make of that?

DONNIE: Disny bother me. Maybe a wee bit divine intervention's just what this bunch of hamsters needs.

RAB: Aww c'mon. As if.

DONNIE: Why no? stranger things happen. Look at this wee blade of grass [Donnie picks one from the ground which must have come off when the ball hit the guy sitting next to him – the loudspeaker said the guy would be fine, well, after the

The Argument from Design

emergency dentist's finished with him anyway]. Look at how nice it is. Look at a' they wee veins. Delicate and precious it is. Perfectly suited tae its place in life.

RAB: [gives Donnie a *very* funny look] An' your point is ... ?

DONNIE: Well c'mon. This just happened eh? Just pure an' utter chance? This wee dod of grass – perfectly pit the gither. Doin' its job perfectly ... And nuthin made it?

RAB: A few zillion years of workin' up tae it I believe is the answer tae that.

DONNIE: Away an' work! Ah don't care how long it hud tae get this way it's no just an accident.

RAB: Your point Donnie?

DONNIE: Simple, stands tae reason. Sumthin' must have made it. Sumthin' must have said, right at the beginnin', "Haud oan a wee minute, ah think I'll make a universe". Cos' that's the only way I can see tae explain how everythin's just right for the job.

RAB: You're losing me now pal, yur soundin' like wan of they philophisers. How does that wee bit of grass prove tae you that the Big Man up there *is* up there?

DONNIE: Easy. See this watch. I've seen it come together bit by bit in my back garden these past six years. Every day, a new wee bit just appeared, an' it a' grew intae this watch that you see before your eyes.

RAB: You sure that's jist Bovril you've got there?

DONNIE: This watch is just a total accident.

RAB: Get a grip.

DONNIE: You don't think so, eh?

RAB: Look, it's a complicated wee thing. It's got a million an' wan functions. You don't even know what they a' are cos you never got the instruction book translated out of the Hungarian, cos you bought it cheap aff that dodgy guy in the pub.

DONNIE: [looks around] Shut up. Anyway, you're right. It is really complicated – so sumthin' must have *made* it, sumthin' must have *designed* it, it didny just happen right?

RAB: Obviously.

DONNIE: An' is the entire universe and cosmos no just a wee bit more complicated than this wee watch?

RAB: Aye, but so?

DONNIE: Aww man, pick yer ain brains wi' a cotton bud will ye? This watch is complicated. It could never, ever, never have just happened. It must've been designed, made, pit the gither by someone ... and the universe is a zillion qaudillion times bigger and merr complicated than this watch right? So ... sumthin' must huv designed and made that as well, eh?

RAB: Aye, ye've goat a point there right enough. But jist wan thing. If everything in this big auld universe is designed and made, how come the design for this team we're watching is sae mince?

DONNIE: Another eternal mystery of the infinitesimal cosmos Rab, another eternal mystery . . .

The Argument from Design

Rab and Donnie have just covered one of the oldest "proofs" for the existence of God. The best known version of this argument came from William Paley in the 19th century. He argued that if you came across a watch lying in a field you'd assume that someone had lost it, and that it had a maker somewhere – it didn't come about completely by chance. This is called the **Teleological Argument** or the Argument from Design:

◆ Everything in the universe is just right for its purpose →

◆ This points to the fact that it must have been designed for that purpose →

◆ Things which are designed can only be designed by intelligent beings →

◆ The universe is unimaginably vast and unbelievably complicated →

◆ So, the thing which made it must be too →

◆ Only God could be that thing →

◆ Therefore God must have designed and made it →

◆ Therefore God must exist

Task

You're in the crowd, and you've heard Rab and Donnie's conversation. You turn to your pal and say "Whit aboot that then, eh?". Now write the conversation you have in the same style.

The Anthropic Principle

For many people, just looking around is proof enough that a God exists. The more we find out about nature the more amazing it is.

If planet Earth was just a little closer to the sun then life as we know it would not be possible. It wouldn't be possible if our planet was just a little further from the sun either. It seems like the planet is like baby bear's porridge – "just right". If you're religious then that isn't a surprise – that's God's plan – he made the Earth for us so what else could it be but perfect for us?

This view is called the **Anthropic Principle**. It says that the design of everything is anthropo (mankind) centric (centred on). It shows regularity and order because otherwise life would

The Argument from Design

be impossible. This doesn't just point to a designer, but to a designer who is intelligent. The designer also needs to be very powerful. Who else could that be but God?

For these reasons, religious people talk about two features of design which they say strengthen their argument –

Design qua purpose – this means that everything in the universe seems to be perfectly suited to what it does

Design qua regularity – this means that the universe is full of order instead of disorder. Things are predictable. If it was just up to luck, then things would be a mess.

Could a monkey write Shakespeare?

For example:

Shakespeare's Monkeys

Believers in a designer say that the chance of the universe coming together by chance is just about impossible. It would be like filling a room with monkeys and typewriters . . . eventually one of them would type the entire works of Shakespeare. Not likely is it? Theists believe that the universe coming together by chance is just as unlikely.

Wind-formed Jumbo Jets

Another way of looking at it is this: Theists would say that the possibility of the universe coming together by pure chance is about the same as the chance of a whirlwind blowing through a junkyard and assembling a working jumbo jet out of the stuff lying around.

Faith and Reason

Religious people would say that the Argument from Design can be supported in two ways –

Reason: When you actually think through the amount of "chance" and "good luck" needed to put together a universe without a designer, it's obvious that it couldn't have happened that way

Faith: Religious people believe in a creator (God) for all sorts of other reasons – it's a matter of faith that he designed the universe too.

Task

Discuss: What do you think of the arguments you've heard so far?

Rejecting the design argument

You're walking along the beach – alone. There's no one else around. You see a pebble. Nothing remarkable there. Further on you see two pebbles, one on top of the other. That's interesting, you think to yourself. Soon you come to three pebbles, piled one on top of the other again. Mmmm, curious. As you walk along, you find more piles of stones. The further you go the higher the piles. Of course you wonder who did it (and why). Maybe you're even looking around yourself.

But wait. Why should a pile of pebbles ten high be any stranger than one two-high? Or even more strange to think about, how much more odd is it to find a three-high pile of pebbles than to find a two-high pile? Why can't both be chance? You decide from what you see that the piles "must have been made like that". But that's not the same as having proof that this is so.

Looks designed, but was it?

13

Looks designed = is designed?

The Argument from Design is based on the idea that if something looks designed then it is – and designed by an intelligent designer. However, saying that something *looks* designed doesn't prove that it has been!

Or maybe it's just the way you look at it. A beautiful sunset is only possible because the sun is a massive thermonuclear reactor and almost unimaginably violent. When you look at a beautiful tree remember that it has grown because it crowded out weaker saplings and "stole" their sunlight – letting them die. Is this such an intelligent design?

Perhaps an intelligent design

A bad design?

Many opponents of the Argument from Design say that if the universe was designed, then the design wasn't very good. Pain and suffering, the existence of evil, the cruelty of nature are all examples of bad design. Such a poor design points to a pretty poor designer.

Not enough nipples: The female quoll has only six nipples. But when she gives birth there are usually around 24 in a litter. The "design" seems to involve the need for a struggle between these young – because only six will survive. Their survival is based on the abilities they have been born with (or their design!). This design "requires" 18 of the baby quolls to die.

Dying before you're born: The male of the species called *Acarophenax tribolii* has an interesting life. Its mother produces fifteen eggs. All are female apart from one. The male develops inside his mother's body, mates with his 14 sisters, and then dies before he can ever be born. This is certainly an odd kind of design.

A System where there has to be pain and suffering: To survive, most forms of life on earth depend upon the death of other things. Sometimes these deaths are natural and sometimes they're pretty brutal.

The luck of the draw: Sometimes life seems to be a lottery. People smoke, drink, take all sorts of risks and live until they're 98. Others live careful, healthy lives and die when they're 25. If the universe is designed, it's a bit of a haphazard design.

Some people's experience tells them that the universe must be designed – maybe this is just what they want to think. Maybe their experience has been misunderstood.

Bad Argument?

Some have argued that we don't even need to look at nature to reject the Argument from Design. The argument itself is wrong. The most famous critic of the argument was probably David Hume. He dealt with the argument mainly in – *Dialogues concerning Natural Religion* (1779). Hume makes eight points:

◆ Even if the argument from design was right, it still doesn't prove that God was the designer. It could just as easily have been a different God, or a God we've never heard of. It could just as easily be a being which is the complete opposite to what we think God is.

> ### Task
> Do some research into this issue and find more examples of what seems to be good and bad design

God's council planning the universe

The Argument from Design

◆ Because we think the universe *must have* been designed doesn't prove that it actually was.

◆ If it was designed – who or what designed the designer?

◆ If we believe in a designer because everything seems made, then why wouldn't that designer be like us in other ways? And if he is, then can't he make mistakes?

◆ Why must we think there was *one* God? Why not a team of Gods? Big things tend to be made by more than one person – why not the universe?

◆ Maybe the universe itself is "God". Maybe it "made" itself. It's just as reasonable as saying that God made himself.

◆ Maybe all the order in the universe is just chance. Maybe the laws of physics "organised" the universe into something which looks as if it must have been made. Maybe the laws of physics are God.

◆ Finally, Hume says that the argument from design fails miserably because the universe shows just as many signs of disorder and irregularity as order and regularity. God could have done a better job.

A snowflake

Source A

Neither, secondly, would it invalidate our conclusion, that the watch sometimes went wrong or that it seldom went exactly right. The purpose of the machinery, the design, and the designer might be evident, and in the case supposed, would be evident, in whatever way we accounted for the irregularity of the movement, or whether we could account for it or not. It is not necessary that a machine be perfect in order to show with what design it was made: still less necessary, where the only question is whether it were made with any design at all.

Natural Theology William Paley (1800)

Comments

Paley seems to be replying to the argument that the universe doesn't point to a designer because it doesn't look like it's that well designed. He says that whether something is well made or not has nothing to do with whether it was made or not. Maybe we don't always understand why things are the way they are – maybe things could be a lot more disordered, maybe God's holding things together in ways we can't imagine. Even a watch which doesn't work very well is still a watch, and still shows evidence of a watchmaker. So, what looks like an imperfect universe can still point to a designer.

Source B

When you come to look into this argument from design, it is a most astonishing thing that people can believe that this world, with all the things that are in it, with all its defects, should be the best that omnipotence and omniscience has been able to produce in millions of years. I really cannot believe it. Do you think that, if you were granted omnipotence and omniscience and millions of years in which to perfect your world, you could produce nothing better than the Ku-Klux Klan or the Fascists? Moreover, if you accept the ordinary laws of science, you have to suppose that human life and life in general on this planet will die out in due course: it is a stage in the decay of the solar system . . .

Why I am not a Christian Bertrand Russell
(Unwin Paperbacks 1979. p18)

Comments

Bertrand Russell argues two things. He wonders if the universe is designed, is this the best God could come up with? He suggests that anyone granted the same powers might have made a better job of it all. The design of the universe seems flawed – so flawed that it can't point to any God. He also wonders why a God would bother to create life, when all the science points to the fact that eventually our sun will die and so will life on earth. What's the point?

The Argument from Design

Facts and Figures

◆ Fred Hoyle calculated that the chances of a single bacterium coming together by pure chance is 1 in $10^{40,000}$

◆ Humans are very complex. There are around 15–20 billion neurons in your body

◆ The chances of typing all the 488 letters in Shakespeare's "Shall I compare you to a summer's day?" correctly by doing it randomly is 1 in 10^{690}

Activities

Knowledge and Understanding

Intermediate 1

1 Do this crossword;

Across
2 The _____ from Design (8)
4 Could the universe have come about by this – or the watch? (6)
6 If the universe is designed does it have this? (7)

Down
1 William Paley (and Donnie!) used this to prove there's a designer (5)
3 Donnie used this to show design too (5)
5 The name given to the argument in this section (6)
7 The philosopher who rejected this argument (4)

2 What did William Paley say you'd think if you came across a watch lying in a field?

3 Copy and Complete:

The _____ Principle says that everything in the universe is just _____ for life to exist. This shows that there must be an _____ designer. Religious people say that this designer could only be ___.

God   right   Anthropic   intelligent

4 Religious people (sometimes!) use jumbo jets and typing monkeys as a way of explaining the Argument from Design. How do they do this?

5 In what way might the quoll show that the universe wasn't designed?

6 Choose two of Hume's arguments. Describe them in your own words.

7 Draw up a table with two columns. One is *Evidence for Design*, the other is *Evidence against Design*. Use the information in this section to complete your table.

Activities continued

8 Read Source A and the comments on it again. Does a poorly-made watch prove it wasn't designed? Explain your answer.

9 Read Source B and the comments on it again. What is Russell's argument here?

Intermediate 2

1 Now that you have studied this section, how do you think Donnie could have responded to Rab's last question in a more helpful way?

2 In your own words, describe how William Paley's watchmaker argument is used to "prove" there's a God.

3 In what way does the Anthropic Principle support the existence of a God?

4 What is the difference between *design qua purpose* and *design qua regularity*?

5 How might a religious person argue that the universe could not have come about by pure chance? (hint: monkeys and $10^{40,000}$)

6 Explain how you can't say that the universe *was* designed because it *must have* been designed.

7 Choose one of the examples used under the heading "A bad design?". Describe it in your own words. Now suggest how a religious person might try to argue against this.

8 Which one of Hume's arguments (if any!) do you think is the most convincing? Explain your answer.

9 Read Source A again. What is Paley's point? What do you think of it?

10 Read Source B again. Do you agree with Russell?

11 Does Fred Hoyle's figure support or reject the possibility that the universe was designed? Explain your answer.

Practical Activities

1 Donnie and Rab have now read this chapter of the book. They meet up again at next week's football match. Write the discussion they might have.

2 Design a poster which outlines the arguments used by William Paley. The poster could look like an old-fashioned watch with cogs and springs. You could write the arguments around the rim of the cogs and along the spirals of the springs.

3 Try out some of the incredible levels of probability involved in this section! You could maybe use scrabble pieces for this. Each person in the class should choose one at random. They should then be put together completely at random by selecting individuals to come and put their letter in a row. Give yourself a time limit (a long one would be best). Do any words appear?

4 Create a display in your classroom – "Good World/Bad World?". Cut out examples of newspaper stories/magazine articles which show good and bad things in the world.

5 Design a short information leaflet: "The Argument from Design – for and against". Include the arguments as well as your own opinions.

6 Some people think that if God made the universe he could have done a better job of it. Write three or four things on separate pieces of card which show the kind of things you would do (if you could) to make the world a better place. Display these in your classroom.

EXISTENCE OF GOD

Unit Assessment Question

Intermediate 1; Outcome 1:
How have Christians responded to criticisms of the Argument from Design?

Intermediate 2: Outcome 3:
"The universe shows evidence of having been designed so God must have designed it". Do you agree?

Sample Exam Question

Intermediate 1:
How might a religious person argue that God exists? (4)

Intermediate 2:
How far is the Argument from Design helpful for the religious person? (6)

Homework

Choose one of the examples in this section under the heading "A bad design?". In around 50 words, write a response to it which might be made by a religious person.

Funtime

Flick through this (or any other) book. Open the pages at random and select a word each time. Do this 50 times. See if you can – completely randomly – come up with any sentences which make sense!

The First Cause Argument

Proposing the first cause argument

"What is a hole in the ground?" A hole is a gap in something, or an area of space surrounded by matter, but is it a *thing*? Some would say it isn't, because it's no*thing*, and nothing isn't something. So how can we talk of a hole being a thing? Maybe we shouldn't use the word hole at all and simply describe an absence of space in the ground as . . . an absence of space in the ground. So you could go and dig an absence of space in the ground.

But wait. How can this space be *in* the ground? It's space, it's not any*where*. Now, hang on to your sanity, it's a similar argument. Is it possible to say that there's any*thing* which started off as no*thing*?

More than this, when does the hole stop being a hole? When it's filled in of course. But this change in its state depends upon it being something before. It's now a filled-in hole having been a hole. Is this the same as never having been a hole at all? How do we know that all areas of ground weren't holes in the past . . . Does this hole, not-hole cycle go back forever? Read on . . .

St Thomas Aquinas' Argument

Aquinas (1224–1274) argued that the existence of the universe proves that there was a creator God, because how else could everything have begun?

◆ Everything that happens is caused by something else. Things just don't pop into existence without a whole series of events coming before them to bring them into existence. Aquinas said that everything has to be "moved" or changed by something else

◆ This whole series of events must have started off somewhere and somehow

Task

Two workies are standing around the hole discussing whether a hole in the ground is something or nothing? Write the conversation they might have about this.

21

The First Cause Argument

When is a hole a hole?

◆ This means that there has to be a point where everything started

◆ At this point there must have been *something*, instead of *nothing*, because something can't come from nothing

◆ There must therefore have been a First Cause of all things

◆ This thing couldn't itself have been caused by anything else, so it must be pretty powerful

◆ The only thing which meets the requirements is what we call God

◆ Therefore God exists.

Contingent and Necessary Beings

Aquinas argued that beings are generally *contingent*. This means that they depend on other things for their existence. For example, you are contingent upon your Mum and Dad. Every living thing is contingent upon another. The trouble with this is that it means you go could go back forever. This is called *infinite regress*.

Many religious people think this doesn't make any sense at all. Somewhere along the line there has to be a being (or beings) which isn't contingent.

A being like this is called a *necessary* being. It is uncreated – it couldn't even have created itself. Aquinas argued that the only being capable of this would be what we call God. This makes God the Necessary Being.

Task

Explain Aquinas' argument in your own words. What do you think of it?

God, the Necessary being

The Leibniz version

Gottfried Leibniz (1646–1716) pointed out another feature of the First Cause argument by asking two very simple questions:

a Why does anything exist at all?

b Given that things exist, why do they exist in the form that they do?

He was saying that it is just as likely that nothing could exist as that anything exists. This suggests that there's a point to it all, and that something started it off. This thing couldn't have been started off by anything else, because then that would need a creator and so on backwards forever. So, there must be a First Cause. This is God.

Faith or Reason?

You may need to make your own mind up here! Religious people would argue that the First Cause argument can be based on both:

Faith: To say that God is the uncaused First Cause of everything else which happens can't be proved. You have to accept it as a matter of faith. But it's not blind faith, it's quite sensible because ...

Reason: It just doesn't make any sense to say that things go back causing each other for all eternity. A far more reasonable thing to do is to decide that at some point something must have kicked it off.

Ockham's Razor

Ockham's Razor says; we should always try to answer a question in the simplest way possible. It's far more neat and tidy to believe that there was a First Cause than to believe there wasn't. To suggest a First Cause (God) is a lot simpler.

The Big Bang – does it help?

For many years, people who didn't believe in a First Cause could argue that everything in the universe could be eternal. Maybe it has just always existed. The Big Bang theory (see pages 107–109) points to a moment when everything began. Many religious people liked this because it seemed to support the idea of a First Cause.

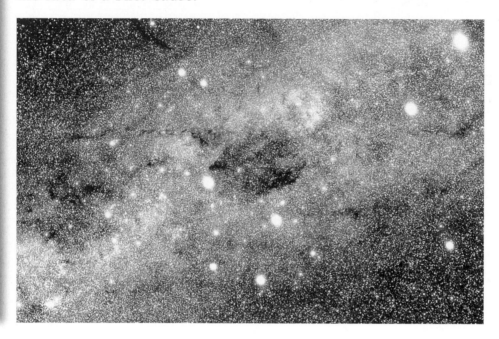

It all began with a Big Bang

But the Big Bang theory says that, not only did everything begin at the Big Bang, space and time did too. If God caused the Big Bang, where and when did he do it? Was (and is) he outside of space and time? And if he is, how can he be a part of everyday life?

Task

In what ways does the Big Bang theory help/hinder the First Cause argument?

Rejecting the first cause argument
A scientific approach

Could something have just started without being caused? According to science, yes (probably). The theory of quantum physics deals with the sub-atomic world. Things at this level are very unpredictable. If the theory is right, then particles just appear for no reason and without any cause. Niels Bohr, showed that quantum physics is unpredictable. Things can come from nothing without any apparent cause – at the subatomic level. If everything is made of atoms (and smaller particles) then maybe anything can appear out of nothing – even universes. Bohr said, "Anyone who is not shocked by quantum theory has not understood it". There are still debates and arguments about this theory, but, if it is true, then it destroys the need for any first cause.

Another bad argument?

Before the amazing findings of quantum physics there were attacks on the argument itself.

Because everything we see has a cause, does this mean that all things have to have the same cause? The philosopher Bertrand Russell said that every human has a mother, but that doesn't mean that the human race has to have a mother. Even if everything in the universe has a cause, it doesn't follow that the universe itself must have a cause too.

Why can't the Universe be *infinite*? Just because we can't get our heads round the idea of something existing for all eternity doesn't mean it hasn't.

So there's no solid reason why the universe can't have always existed. That's no more unbelievable than that it just came into existence out of absolutely nothing.

The argument trips itself up. It says that everything must have had a cause. Then it says that there must have been a first cause which had no cause. This is a contradiction. You can't

Who created human life?

The First Cause Argument

say that everything must have had a cause ... except for ... It makes no sense.

Even if we accept that there must have been a first cause, it's a giant leap of belief from saying that to saying it was God. Also, it doesn't prove that this God is still around. Maybe the effort of being a first cause was so great that the being ceased to exist afterwards.

So, if we accept the need for a first cause, why does it have to be God? If God can be uncaused, why can't the universe? It's just as likely. Maybe the universe itself is God.

And why not?

Religious people might say that although the First Cause argument might be a bit wobbly, when you put it together with other things, it supports the idea that God exists. They would say that the universe exists for a purpose, it's not "just an accident". If life has meaning and purpose, then it matters how you live it – and there's some point to each one of us.

They might also argue the other way round – if you can accept that the universe caused itself, why can't you accept that God did it instead? Religious people would then turn to other arguments to support their belief in God – making God the First Cause seem more likely than not.

Task

Explain your own views about the First Cause argument using the evidence above.

Source A

In the observable world causes are found to be ordered in series; we never observe, nor ever could, something causing itself, for this would mean it preceded itself, and this is not possible. Such a series of causes must stop somewhere ... Now if you eliminate a cause you also eliminate its effects ... so that you cannot have a last cause unless you have a first ... One is therefore forced suppose some first cause, to which everyone gives the name "God".

Summa Theologiae Thomas Aquinas

Comments

This is Aquinas' key argument. It is based on the fact that, if something caused itself, it would have to have existed before it existed! So there must, logically, be something which has no beginning. Aquinas lived in a world where quantum physics wasn't even heard of and so it's quite reasonable for him to argue that you can't ever see something being caused by nothing. To leap from the existence of the universe to a First Cause God isn't all that difficult.

Source B

The argument that there must exist a first cause of everything is open to serious doubt so long as we adhere to any simple notion of cause, irrespective of whether the universe is infinitely old, or had a definite beginning in time. Exotic causal mechanisms, such as reversed-time causality or quantum mental processes might conceivably remove the need for a prior cause of creation. Nevertheless one is still left with a feeling of unease . . . Although we may be able to find a cause for every event (unlikely in view of quantum effects), still we would be left with the mystery of why the universe has the nature it does, or why there is any universe at all.

Paul Davies *God and The New Physics*
(Penguin 1983 pp 42–43)

Comments

Davies shows that science hasn't got one solid conclusion about whether a first cause is needed or not. He begins and ends this book with the statement that he believes that "science offers a surer path than religion in the search for God". His (sometimes very complicated) argument returns in this source to the idea of mystery. The more science unfolds the structure of the universe, the more amazing it seems – the more it points to something "out there". He claims that the reason he wrote this book was that he is convinced that there's more to the world than meets the eye.

- ◆ Quantum Theory says that light behaves like waves, but also behaves like solid matter (particles)

- ◆ The famous Schrodinger's Cat experiment suggests that, until observed, the cat in the box is between life and death

- ◆ It would take 10 million atoms side by side to stretch 1mm (and atoms are mostly empty space!)

Facts and Figures

Activities

Knowledge and Understanding

Intermediate 1

1 Do you think a hole in the ground is something or nothing? Explain!

2 Here's Thomas Aquinas' First Cause argument. Copy the true statements only.
   a Everything which happens must have been caused
   b Nothing caused everything
   c The chain of causes must have started somewhere
   d Nothing can come from something
   e Something can come from nothing
   f Something can't come from nothing
   g There could not have been a First Cause
   h There must have been a First Cause
   i This must be very powerful
   j It must be the universe
   k It must be God

EXISTENCE OF GOD

Activities continued

3 What is a *contingent* being?
 a One which depends on nothing else for its existence
 b One which depends on something else for its existence

4 What is a *necessary* being?
 a One which depends on nothing else for its existence
 b One which depends on something else for its existence

5 Leibniz asked these two questions. Write them out correctly.
 a anything Why exist all at does?
 b Given exist things that do, exist why form the in they that do do?

6 Copy and complete:
Quantum _____ deals with the ___ _____ world. Things at this level are very _____. This means that things can just _____ for no reason and without any _____. _____ didn't believe it. He said, God does not play _____. But if quantum theory is true, then maybe the universe didn't need a _____ _____.

Theory	unpredictable	sub-atomic
appear	cause	dice	Einstein
First	Cause		

7 For the following three statements choose a correct answer from the list below.
 a "Everything needs a cause. God is uncaused". Explain why this statement is a contradiction.
 b "Even if God was the first cause, this tells us nothing about what God might be like" What does this mean?
 c Why might a religious person want to believe in a First Cause?

 Possible answers:
 i Because God is good
 ii Because God must have been caused too then
 iii It means that it could have been anything, not God
 iv It means that there could have been lots of gods
 v It means that the universe itself could be what we call God
 vi Because it's hopeful
 vii Because it makes life more meaningful
 viii Because it means he'll go to heaven
 ix Because it is wrong

8 Read Source A again. How does Aquinas "prove" that something couldn't cause itself?

9 Read Source B again. Why does Davies still have a "feeling of unease"?

Intermediate 2

1 In your opinion, is a hole in the ground nothing or something? Explain your answer.

2 In eight bullet points, write your own version of St Thomas Aquinas' First Cause argument.

3 What's the difference between a contingent being and a necessary being? Which are you?

4 Do you agree that there has to be a necessary being? Explain.

5 How did Leibniz get from the fact that life exists to the belief that God exists?

6 Why might some people think it's "less messy" to believe in God than not to believe in God?

7 Does the Big Bang Theory help the First Cause argument? Explain.

8 Does quantum theory help the First Cause argument? Explain.

9 Choose two of the parts of the first cause argument. Show how they can be rejected.

10 Why might a religious person think the First Cause argument matters?

11 Read Source A again. Give your own explanation of Aquinas' argument in this source.

12 Read Source B again. From your reading of this, do you think Paul Davies is a religious person? Give reasons for your opinion.

Practical Activities

1 Have a class debate: "A hole in the ground isn't anything".

2 How contingent are you? Work out (as far back as you can) how many people you're contingent upon.

3 Find out more about Quantum Theory. Design a poster about it. Show how it can affect basic beliefs about the world a well as the origin of the universe, and the First Cause argument.

4 Remember Rab and Donnie from the last section? Imagine they meet up at the next game. This time they decide to chat about the First cause argument (their team's becoming painful to watch!). In the same style, write the conversation they might have.

5 Do you think life would change if the First Cause argument was shown to be true? How? Discuss in your class and then make a note of your findings. What would be the implications for your life if it was proved that there was a First Cause? What about the opposite? Would your life change if it was proved that there was no First Cause?

6 Find out more about the life and work of two of the following. Prepare a short report on your findings.

Thomas Aquinas
Niels Bohr
Gottfried Leibniz
Albert Einstein

Unit Assessment Question

Intermediate 1: Outcome 2:
Explain how a Christian might defend the First Cause argument.

Intermediate 2 – Outcome 3:
"The First Cause argument is a failure"

To what extent do you agree?

Sample Exam Question

Intermediate 1:
Outline the First Cause argument. (4)

Intermediate 2:
How helpful is the First Cause argument in supporting belief in God? (6)

Homework

Explain the First Cause argument to two people you know. Ask them what they think of it. Write a 50 word report on their answers.

Funtime

Do your own strip cartoon version of the arguments covered in this section.

Religious Experience: The Case For God

Jamie is 17. Last night, sitting outside, looking up at the night sky he had a strange feeling. He suddenly felt at peace. He felt at one with the whole universe. He felt as if there was some real point to his life.

Hannah is 43. Last night she woke from sleep to find that a bright shining figure was standing at the bottom of her bed. He told her he was God and that she had a message to deliver to the world. Then he dissolved and disappeared.

Nikki is 27. Last night she was driving home in the dark on a quiet country road. Strange lights appeared above the car. Her car's power failed and came to a halt. She got out to see a UFO move slowly over her car and away – fast – into the night sky.

Julie is 30. Last night, when she was in church she felt that God was speaking to her. She didn't hear anything but just felt his presence. She doesn't know what to make of it, but is keeping quiet about it for the moment.

Emma is 72. Her husband died a year ago. She still has his chair in the living room. Last night she saw him sitting in it, smiling at her.

Francis is 40. His mother died ten years ago, but every night he still speaks to her, and he hears her speaking back.

Tom is 62. He's a Christian Minister. He always feels that God is with him. He feels that God shows him the right way to live.

Elizabeth is 50. Last night she went to a Christian meeting. There was lots of music and plenty of emotion. At the end she gave her life to Jesus and felt filled with the spirit of God.

Dean is 27. He's just out of prison for attempted murder. A few years ago, God spoke to him in a dream. Dean became a Christian and has changed completely from his old self.

Religious experience

What is a religious experience?

If the stories above were real (they're not), which one(s) would you believe?

Many religious people would say that the arguments you've looked at so far – the Argument from Design and First Cause argument – don't prove anything. The only thing which can prove that God is real is experience.

This experience causes a change in your life which is so great that it must have some divine cause. They say that instead of trying to find God with your head alone, you should also use your heart. Religious experiences can take many forms:

A feeling of "one-ness" with everything. This is a feeling of being part of something bigger – of there being more to life than meets the eye. Maybe you're at the beach watching the oceans crash onto the shore. Maybe you're sitting in your class. Sometimes this is called an experience of the *numinous* – the mystery that is the universe.

An experience following some major event in your life. This can flood you with emotions and cause you to experience things in a very different way. It makes you look at yourself differently and maybe lead your life differently too. People who have survived death – when others around them haven't – often feel that this means their life has a new meaning. They feel that they have survived for a reason.

A cleaner at the World Trade Centre took a holiday two weeks early. She was on holiday during the attack on 11 September 2001. It was only a year later that she found out that she had been mistakenly named as one of the dead. She said that her escape from this tragedy has made her feel that there's some purpose to her life.

Sometimes the experiences are more direct. Instead of a general feeling, some people claim to have heard or seen God, or Jesus, or Angels. Usually it's completely unexpected. But it's almost always life-changing in one way or another. It may seem to be a response to something – a question asked or a prayer said.

Sometimes it happens to people whose lives are in a bit of a mess. It might happen during religious worship or when your senses are somehow more alert than usual. Sometimes it happens in really odd places – like on the top deck of a double-decker bus.

Sometimes these experiences are linked with strange events. For example, a religious experience might be accompanied by some kind of miracle.

Task

Have you or anyone you know had anything which could be called a religious experience? Discuss in your class.

Religious experiences can happen anywhere

Proof of God?

Do religious experiences prove that there's a God? For the people who have them, probably. But what about the rest of us? If someone says that they've had a religious experience, should that be enough proof for the rest of us to believe it?

Do you need proof to believe?

What if someone in your class told you that they'd had pizza for dinner last night. You'd probably believe them. But if they told you it was delivered having been oven-baked in the heat of a volcano in Hawaii, then you might be less trusting.

The more extreme a claim, the less likely we are to believe it. But then what's extreme? Lots of people will believe it when someone says they've seen a ghost. But the same people will have their doubts about an experience of God. Why? Maybe it's because some people already doubt the existence of God and so when such a religious experience is reported to them, they don't believe it because they don't believe in God in the first place! How sensible is that?

Proof doesn't have to be scientific. You can't scientifically prove that you feel love towards another person. So why should there be a need to prove that a person has experienced God?

The role of the soul

Anyway, maybe a religious experience doesn't happen in the same way that other experiences do. When someone is happy you can show, using a brain scan, which areas of the brain are in action. You can also see them smile, hear them laugh and so on. But religious experiences might only be experienced by your spirit or soul. So far, souls and spirits have cleverly dodged scientific investigation. So, if we can't get hold of the soul, how can we know what it might be experiencing?

Science can't even decide if the mind is the same thing as the brain – so how can it investigate religious experiences in your soul?

Task

What do you think of the idea of a soul? Get your class to anonymously write their views about the existence of a soul on a scrap of paper and display them.

33

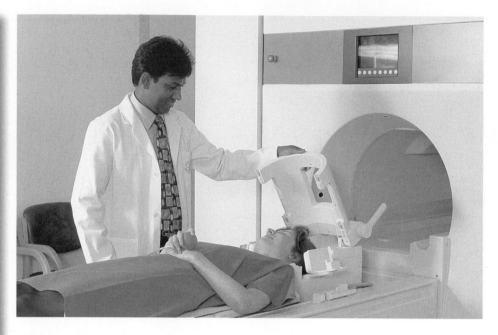

Science can identify emotional responses

How do we know anything?

Someone tells you they love you. You don't ask for proof. The experience you have of their love is enough. You know how they make you feel and how you're different with them. This is enough experience for your purposes. When you step into a car you have faith in its mechanics – your life depends upon it. But you have enough experience of cars (which work) to know that it's not an act of blind trust.

How much do we trust our senses and how often are they right?

Our daily experience is full of "filtering". Every day you might see a few hundred different people. You filter out what you

Task

Without looking, describe everything that's on the walls in your classroom.

Now describe exactly what the teacher you had last period was wearing.

How different are the responses given by the people in your class?

Perception: rabbit or duck

want/need to know and ignore the rest. Perhaps religious experiences are where people have paid attention to the experience and gained something from it. Maybe it just depends how you look at it. Does the diagram show a rabbit? Maybe you've had religious experiences but just didn't know it.

Task

Discuss the good and bad points of "just accepting" religious experiences like this.

Just say Yes

In many faiths throughout the world they don't even bother trying to prove the existence of God by argument. They say you should believe what you *feel* is right and true. If you have an experience which suggests there is a God, then why do you have to analyse it, why not just accept it?

Proof of the pudding?

Many religious people say that there is solid proof that religious experience is real and points to the existence of a God. Their argument is simple; It must be real because it brings about changes in people that otherwise would never have happened.

Task

Do you think these experiences prove there's a God? Discuss and note down the range of views expressed.

Paul works for the Bethany Christian Trust in Edinburgh. This helps drug-addicts and alcoholics to kick their addiction. It also teaches them about the Christian faith. Paul says that he has seen people without any religious faith come off drugs and alcohol . . . but he's never seen such people stay off them. However, everyone he's seen changed by a religious experience has stayed away from their addiction and become well-adjusted people.

Cammy had an alcohol problem as a young person in Paisley. For seven years he drank and took drugs daily. He was, in his own words, "a vicious thug". He attacked his step-father with a hammer – almost killing him. This was because his step-father was beating Cammy's mother. Cammy escaped prison because his mum took the blame. He was arrested soon after for carrying out three serious assaults in one night. Eventually he was imprisoned for stabbing a man and leaving him for dead in Paisley town centre.

On release he got a job driving a taxi (even though he was still regularly "stoned out of his mind"). A woman got into his cab and told him that she'd had a message "from the other side". She told him, "A dark cloud is hanging over your life. Only God can save you from it". Cammy is now a Minister of the Church of Scotland in Haddington, East Lothian.

Religious Experience – The Case For God

More humdrum?

Those who knew these people would have seen a big change. They wouldn't doubt that something real had happened. But not all religious experience is big drama. Some religious people feel that their experience of God is a lot "quieter" and more restrained.

Some people just feel that God is with them in their daily lives, and always has been. He's a constant presence, not a blinding light. Some Christians believe that this was what Jesus experienced. Not a sudden realisation that he had a special relationship with God – but a constant feeling of God's presence.

More evidence?

Religious experiences seem common throughout the world – no matter what the faith or circumstances. In Islam, the Prophet Muhammed's experience of the revelation of the Qur'an is the starting-point of the Muslim faith. In Buddhism, the Enlightenment of Siddartha Gautama is the moment when this faith began. Siddartha's Enlightenment was itself a religious experience. It transcended (went beyond) the normal everyday experiences of life.

Even outside religion, experience of the numinous can lead to great life-changes. The experience of the power of nature led people like John Muir to care for the environment because of its powers to "restore the human spirit". All of these are examples of conversion.

With so many examples of experiences like this throughout the world and throughout time, you really have to wonder if they do point to something.

Modern views

Many psychologists and scientists have explored religious experience. William James is probably the most well-known. In his book, *The Varieties of Religious Experience* (1902), he describes the features of a religious experience:

◆ The experience is usually very short. You couldn't really function normally if you were "high" like this all the time!

◆ You can't stop it. It's not something you choose to happen – it just does. Sometimes it's completely unexpected

◆ It gives you a new look at something in life – a new insight. This might help you understand life better

◆ You can't describe the experience. It can only be understood by someone who's gone through the same kind of thing.

Task

Discuss: Can you see any problems with letting scientists investigate alleged religious experiences?

The Humanistic Psychologists, like Maslow and Rogers, said that to be a "fully-functioning person" you have to reach a point called "self-actualisation". This is a transcendent awareness of the unity of things – not that different to a religious experience. This is the high spot in human development. The same group of psychologists also said that people have "peak episodic experiences". These are flashes of heightened awareness – not that different to a religious experience.

The Alister Hardy Research Centre in Oxford is devoted to looking into religious experiences. It has so far researched thousands of cases –could they all be wrong?

Source A

There is a vast continuum of forms and degrees of . . . religious experience, ranging from the powerful and continuous sense of God's presence . . . to a very ordinary and fleeting sense of the reality of God experienced by ordinary people in moments of prayer and meditation, or when reading the scriptures, or when confronted with the vastness and mystery of the universe . . . There are also peak experiences, unforgettably vivid and moving moments of awareness of being in God's unseen presence. One is not alone in this matter . . . down the ages and today; and for some it is the world-wide multitude of those who have experienced and do experience our human life as being lived in the universal presence of God.

John Hick in M Goulder and J Hick *Why Believe in God?* (SCM Press 1983 p 46)

Comments

This book is a dialogue between two friends – one a Christian and one not. Michael Goulder – the other person in the book – is an atheist who used to be a priest. John Hick, still a religious person, describes some features of religious experience here, showing the many different ways in which they might be started off. He's suggesting that the fact that so many people have had them down through the ages means it can't just be coincidence – it must be something more. The more people who have them, the more believable they should be.

Source B

I remember the night, and almost the very spot on the hill-top, where my soul opened out, as it were, into the Infinite, and there was a rushing together of the two worlds, the inner and the outer. It was deep calling unto deep – the deep that my own struggle had opened up within being answered by the unfathomable deep without, reaching beyond the stars. I stood alone with Him who had made me, and all the beauty of the world, and love, and sorrow, and even temptation. I did not seek Him, but felt the perfect unison of my spirit with His. The ordinary sense of things around me faded. For the moment nothing but an ineffable joy and exaltation remained. It is impossible fully to describe the experience. I could not any more have doubted that He was there than that I was. Indeed, I felt myself to be, if possible, the less real of the two.

An example of a religious experience quoted in William James *Varieties of Religious Experience* (1902)

Comments

This quote is one of many in William James' famous book. It is a typical religious experience. It was had by a Priest. This particular experience is half-way between what you could call the numinous and a direct experience of God. It shows many of the features James talks about. For example, the person states quite clearly that he can't describe the experience.

Facts and Figures

◆ The French philosopher, Teilhard de Chardin (1881–1955) described the Noosphere – a "planetary thinking network" or global self-awareness

◆ Around 1 in 8 Americans claim to have had some kind of spiritual experience

◆ Electrically stimulating the temporal lobes of the brain has led to people "hearing" voices and "seeing" things which weren't there

---

Activities

Knowledge and Understanding

Intermediate 1

1 Choose three of the people in the Box at the start of this section (page 30). Write one question you would ask each of them.

2 For each of the people in this box give them a score on a sliding scale of 1–10. 1 = you absolutely never could believe what this person has said, 10 = you absolutely could believe what this person has said, 5 = you're neutral about this person's statement etc.

3 What do you think people mean when they say you should try to find God with your heart?

4 Match up the beginning of these sentences with their endings:

Beginnings
a   The numinous is a feeling of
b   Some people might have a religious experience following

Activities continued

c Religious experiences usually make people
d Sometimes people actually see
e Religious experiences can happen
f A miracle sometimes accompanies

Endings
1 God.
2 feel that their life has special meaning.
3 "one'ness" with everything.
4 almost anywhere at any time.
5 a religious experience.
6 a major event in their life.

5 Would you believe someone who told you they'd seen a ghost? Explain.

6 What if the same person told you they'd seen God. What would you think of that? Explain.

7 If a religious experience happens to your soul – why does this make it hard to prove?

8 Choose one of the boxed stories on page 35. For each one, explain whether you think this is proof of God or not.

9 If someone said that their experience of God was "quieter", what would they mean?
a There wasn't a lot of noise
b God whispered
c God is with them in their daily lives

10 Give one example of a religious experience from a religion other than Christianity.

11 Choose one of the features of a religious experience described by William James on pages 36–37. Write this in your own words.

12 Read Source A again. Give one example of a kind of religious experience which this source describes.

13 Read Source B again. Which of James' features on pages 36–37 does this Source describe?

Intermediate 2

1 Choose three of the people in the box on page 30. Imagine you had to interview them about their experience. Write a set of questions you would ask each one of them.

2 Go through this box. Explain which of the stories you would believe and which you wouldn't believe. Give reasons for your answer.

3 Why might some religious people say that religious experience is the most powerful argument for the existence of God?

4 Explain what is meant by the numinous.

5 Explain how some people believe a religious experience might give their life meaning.

6 Why might someone find it hard to believe that you had seen God?

7 Describe fully why some people would argue that science could never prove whether or not a religious experience is real.

8 What problems could there be if you just accepted a religious experience as true without questioning it?

9 Choose one of the boxed situations on page 35. List as many possible alternative explanations as you can for the change in the person's life.

10 What kind of religious experience might a Christian say Jesus had?

11 How does the amount of religious experiences through time and across the world help the argument that religious experiences are true?

12 Summarise the features of a religious experience according to William James.

13 Read Source A again. What is the argument used by Hick in support of religious experience?

14 Read Source B again. What other explanations might there be for this man's experience?

Practical Activities

1 Choose one of the people in the box on page 30. Using the questions in the Knowledge and Understanding section (Q1), write the dialogue which might follow.

2 If you have ever had an experience like any of the experiences described in this section, write about it. If not, write about a time when you really had a think about the big questions in life.

3 Many religious experiences produce responses which are artistic or poetic. Using artwork or poetry, how might you describe what is meant by the numinous?

4 Using newspapers, magazines, the Internet . . . create a collage of images which illustrate "strange experiences".

5 Do some research in your class. Has anyone ever had an experience they can't explain? How common are "religious experiences" in your school?

6 Look up William James on the Internet. Find other examples of religious experience he uses. Write a brief report on his findings and ideas.

Unit Assessment Question

Intermediate 1: Outcome 2:
Some people think religious experience is not enough proof for the existence of God. How might a religious person respond to this?

Intermediate 2: Outcome 3:
"Religious Experience is all in the mind". How far do you agree?

Sample Exam Question

Intermediate 1:
How might a religious person argue that religious experience is the best proof of the existence if God? (4)

Intermediate 2:
"Religious experience gives the proof needed for belief in God". How far do you agree? (6)

Homework

Imagine you had a dramatic religious experience tonight. In 50 words, describe how your life might change – especially how those who know you might react.

Funtime

In an episode of the Simpson's called "Homer the Heretic", Homer has a religious experience. If you can, watch this video and write about how Homer's religious experience is shown to be "true". If you can't get the video – write your own script outline for an episode where Homer has a religious experience!

Religious Experience: The Case Against God

In the film *Star Trek IV – the Voyage Home*, Mr Spock (who died at the end of Star Trek III) is rescued having been brought back to life by a device called the Genesis Project. Dr McCoy asks Spock what it was like to be dead. Spock replies that they can't discuss it, because they have "no common frame of reference". McCoy is annoyed – "So you're telling me that I have to die before your can discuss this with me". Spock raises an eyebrow in agreement. The argument is simple. Spock's experience of death is so unique that it can only be properly understood by someone who had gone through the same thing.

Star Trek's Spock and McCoy

Way too personal

Religious experiences are often criticised because they're too personal to properly discuss and examine. They are too subjective. You can't get into someone's head to feel what they do – so you can't prove that what they're telling you is true. When I see the colour red, the only way that I know this is red is if we both agree that what we're looking at *is* red. Although

Task

Imagine Spock decides to tell McCoy. Draw a cartoon to explain what he describes. You may need the help of a Trekkie here!

Experience is personal

we agree, I can't know *how* you experience red, and vice-versa. If the experience is something which has only happened to you and not me, then this means it's even harder for me to grasp what you're claiming has happened. The major problem with religious experience is that it is difficult to prove.

Science works on a principle called *verifiability*. This means that something can only be investigated by science if there can be a way found to show that it's true. It's only scientifically proven if it is – or can be – verifiable. Most religious experiences aren't verifiable in the usual way. It's very unlikely that a scientist is going to follow someone around with a whole pile of scientific equipment in the hope that he'll catch them having a religious experience. Anyway, what equipment could the scientist use?

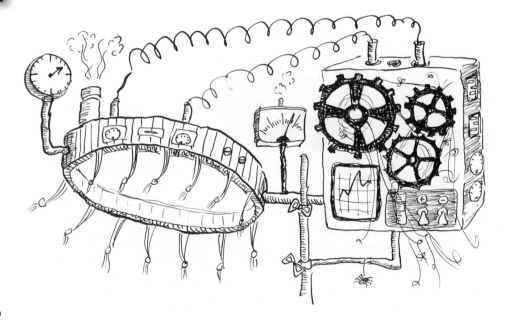

A 'soul-testing' machine

So, if there's no way of proving or disproving a religious experience, how believable can they be? For this reason, many scientists don't accept that religious experiences are proof of the existence of God. They're interesting, and they might tell us something about how the mind/brain works – but they would be a funny way for God to prove his existence.

Task

Discuss: Can you always believe your eyes?

Suppose you come across a creature called a thurglemeeblob. You've never seen one, you don't know what to feed it, or how to look after it. No-one does. There's nothing to compare it to. You can't say very much that's useful about it. Now, suppose that not only is it the only one of its kind, it's completely invisible (except to you). It's a very personal thing. In some ways, you might as well not bother talking about it, because it's unique to you. How different is this from a religious experience?

The soul again

Many religious experiences are "spiritual experiences". If this is true, then again they're not verifiable. The area of the spiritual is outside what science can test. We're back to relying on the person's own report of their experience ... Humanists are atheists. They don't believe that there is such a thing as a soul. In their opinion, spiritual experiences are just things which have other rational explanations, or no explanation yet.

A Thurglemeeblob

All in the mind

The Psychologist, Sigmund Freud, suggested that religious experiences had their origins in the mind. They can't be proved or tested (but then neither can many of Freud's theories like the id, ego and superego!). Freud suggested that religious experiences weren't proof of God, they were just proof of human need. He said:

Freud claimed God was a coping mechanism

Religious experiences are *wish-fulfilment.* This means that we want things like God to be true because it is then a belief we can lean on when things are difficult. Freud said that we all face problems in our lives. To help us through these our mind creates ways to cope. One of these is creating the belief that there's something out there looking after us. Religious people want to believe in God, because otherwise they are afraid of life having no meaning.

God is a *projection* of a perfect father figure. Freud said that our parents have a big influence over our whole lives. Many of our hang-ups come from problems in our childhood. Being human, many parents aren't perfect. We want them to be. Some people then imagine that there must be a perfect parent somewhere and so they create this imaginary parent and give it immense power. Then they call it God.

God is a projection of our ideal self. In short, God's a perfect hero. We look up to others for help in being our best selves – but our heroes are usually imperfect in some way. So, we create in our minds a perfect idea of what we'd like to be – with no flaws. Then we can always look up to God as an example of how we should be. In some ways, this is odd because the God of the Bible does sometimes show what could be called imperfections. He gets angry (and floods the earth), he changes his mind, he does some strange things (like making Abraham almost sacrifice his own son).

The Humanistic psychologist, Carl Rogers, said that the key to being mentally healthy is that your life is full of what he called *unconditional positive regard.* This means that you are loved for who you are – whatever that is. This love has no strings (conditions) attached – it's unconditional. God is something which can always give completely unconditional positive regard (he'll never let you down). Because we all need this, we find it wherever we can – even if it means creating a being in our heads who can always do this for us.

Mind over matter?

Many explanations of religious experience say that we make them happen for ourselves. The human mind/brain is fantastically complex. We still don't understand fully how it works. What we do know is that it can be very powerful. We can consciously or unconsciously create many different states of mind (for many reasons). Maybe we can conjure up for ourselves religious experiences which are so vivid and real that we totally believe they are proof of the existence of a God.

The power of suggestion: Many people are very suggestible. This means that if they can be convinced something is true, they'll actually believe it is – without any real evidence. Many religious experiences happen when the person is very emotional.

If someone is in a state of heightened awareness, then they might be more likely to have a religious experience than when sitting eating their cornflakes watching breakfast TV. Suggestion could also explain miraculous healing events. It is well-known that people can be cured of all sorts of things by the placebo effect. Maybe religious experience is the same.

Altered state of consciousness: Many religious experiences might happen when people are in an "altered state". This just means

Task

Discuss: What do you think of the arguments from these psychologists? Have they any more proof than religious people?

GOD EXISTS

I BELIEVE!

The power of suggestion

Emotional worship

that their brain chemistry is muddled up. Maybe the person's gone through a scary or very emotional experience. Maybe they're ill. Maybe they've been using drugs. In all of these cases, hallucinations are common. What's happening is that the brain is making odd connections. This results in having odd experiences. People who have been close to death often report seeing God or hearing the voices of loved ones who have died

Whipping up the emotions: Many religious experiences happen during religious worship. This is often powerful. There may be rhythmic sound or movement. Long periods of being talked at (maybe to tell you how bad you are and how you can be healed), and there's pressure from others to conform to what's expected of you.

> ### Task
> Imagine you're a religious person. How would you respond to these criticisms of religious experiences?

Proof of the Pudding 2

In the last section it was suggested that religious experiences must be true because they change people for the better. There are many cases of people having religious experiences and then going on to do some pretty nasty stuff.

David Koresh's ranch in Waco, Texas

Case Study: David Koresh

Born in 1959, his mother was then just 14. His stepfather was harsh. Koresh was bullied at school. Shy and quiet, he had a hard childhood. He read the Bible like other kids did comics. At 19 he had a relationship with a 16 year old girl who had his child. But she'd have nothing to do with him. He buried himself deeper in his religion. He began to have powerful feelings that God was telling him he was special – a new Messiah. He became a powerful preacher and gathered a large following.

They lived in a ranch in Waco, Texas, calling themselves "Branch Davidians". But there were many claims that he abused members physically and mentally, and that he had sex with under-age girls. Eventually, the FBI moved in on the Waco ranch. After a long stand-off, on 19 April 1993, the siege ended in fire and a gun battle. 81 people, including Koresh, died. The nine survivors said that Koresh had ordered his followers to die rather than surrender.

Case Study: Reverend Jim Jones

Born in 1931 to a poor family, Jones became a powerful preacher. He was soon claiming the power to heal and that God was directing him in all that he did. He too gained a large following. Very soon though Jones was doing all sorts of nasty stuff – much of it sexual, some of it very violent. By the mid 1970s he had set up a camp in Guyana which he named Jonestown. In November 1978, he ordered his followers to commit suicide at this camp. More than 900 of them, including Jones, did so.

EXISTENCE OF GOD

Of course, it could be that these people didn't have any kind of religious experience – they were just completely nuts. But they certainly seemed to believe that their experience was real – what they did about it was their own choice. But if we use the examples of Jones and Koresh to prove that there's a God you can understand why religious people might object. If we accept religious experience as proof of God when it produces good results, why don't we reject it as proof of God when it seems to end up in bad things happening?

Task

Do the David Koresh and Jim Jones stories prove there's no God?

Too big a jump?

Anyway, even if people do have strange experiences which they call religious, isn't it too big a jump from these to saying that God exists? There can be many other explanations for what we call religious experiences.

Scientists can show how many religious experiences have perfectly rational explanations – from brain chemistry changes to mind-altering drugs to the power of suggestion. Once you add in all of these other explanations for religious experiences, you're left with very few which are unexplained. That's just because there isn't an explanation . . . yet. But to go from the lack of an explanation to the idea that God exists is just too big a jump.

No experience

If we say religious experience *is* proof of God, does that mean *not* having a religious experience is proof that God *doesn't* exist? Many people have not had any religious experience at all. Even many religious people will say that they have never had

Many religious people don't have religious experiences

any kind of experience of God – any feeling in their heart or life-changing event. It is just something they believe. Maybe the fact that so many have not had religious experiences should be enough evidence for us that there's no God.

Religious people might argue that religious experiences happen only to those who need them, or to those who really believe – but non-religious people would say that this is just a way to squirm out of the argument. People who don't have religious experiences don't have them because there's no God to make them happen.

Source A

... the universe in fact is not a caring environment. It is indifferent to human feelings. It is impersonal, and at any moment ... It is capable of destroying human life and achievement. How can we face a senseless universe? ... By giving a face to the universe, by making it personal ... we enable ourselves to face up to its terrors and confusions. We create in the imagination (because it does not exist in fact) a father-figure, and we project it into the universe, and live 'as-if' that illusory figure will care for us.

John Bowker *The Sense of God* (Oneworld 1995, p 118)

Comments

Bowker is reporting Freud's theories of projection and wish-fulfilment. The universe is a scary place, so we make up a God to help us cope with it – we want to believe. Bowker (later in the book) criticises Freud's theories because they are based on ideas (like the id, ego, superego) which themselves can't be proven in the normal scientific way. He goes on to say that even if Freud is absolutely right, religious experience is a projection and is just wish-fulfilment – that still does not prove whether or not a God exists in reality.

Source B

... the line of argument that the whole argument from our mental states to something outside us, is a very tricky affair. Even where we admit all its validity, we only feel justified in doing so, I think, because of the consensus of mankind. If there's a crowd in a room and there's a clock in a room, they can all see the clock. The fact that they all see it tends to make them think it's not an hallucination: whereas these religious experiences do tend to be very private.

Bertrand Russell *Why I Am Not a Christian* (Unwin 1979 p 143)

Comments

This is part of a debate between Russell and Father FC Copleston, S.J. Russell also argues that we can't jump from what we feel to the fact that it proves something real out there. Religious experience is too personal to be able to draw very much information from it which can apply always and everywhere. He later states that there's a big difference between feeling that there's a God and there actually being one. He also states that people often have life-changing experiences which change them for the better – but still it's not proof that this was caused by a God.

Facts and Figures

◆ Most of Freud's theories are based on his work with middle-aged, wealthy, Victorian Viennese women

◆ Almost as many people claim to have seen Elvis as claim to have seen God

◆ Koresh is the name of the fourth horseman of the Apocalypse. It signifies death

Activities

Knowledge and Understanding

Intermediate 1

1 What do you think of Mr Spock's reply to Dr McCoy?

2 Copy the following paragraph. Some of the words are in the wrong places. Put it right.

Religious personal are very subjective. This means that they are experiences. You can't get into my science to see what I'm thinking or feeling. Because they are so true, whether they are unique or not can't be tested by head. This means they can't be difficult. It would be very verified to prove a religious experience actually God, This makes it a difficult way to prove that there's a happened.

3 In what way is a thurglemeeblob like a religious experience?

4 Here are Freud's ideas about religious experiences. Match the theory and its explanation:

Theories
Projection
● Wish-fulfilment
● father-figure
● ideal self

Explanations
● We want God to be true so much that we make him up

● We project out what we want to be true
● God is what we'd ideally like to be like
● God becomes for us the perfect parent

5 What is *unconditional positive regard*? Why might someone believe God can give you this?

6 What might someone mean if they say that religious experience is just an example of the power of suggestion?

7 What kinds of things might cause people to have hallucinations?

8 Read the David Koresh case study again. State two things he did which might make you wonder if his "message" was really from God.

9 "It's too big a jump from religious experience to saying God exists" What do you think this means?

10 Many people haven't had religious experiences. What might this do to the argument? Find one correct response from the list below. Which answer do you think is best?
i It could mean that the event is very personal
ii It could mean that God is very choosy

Activities continued

   iii It could mean that God only appears when you're alone

   iv It could mean that you haven't noticed you've had a religious experience

11 Read Source A again. Why might "a senseless universe" make us want to believe in God?

12 Read Source B again. What point is Russell making?

Intermediate 2

1 Explain fully why the subjective nature of religious experience makes it difficult to verify.

2 Do you think there might be any way to test a religious experience? Explain.

3 Do you think some reports of religious experiences might be more believable than others? Explain

4 In what ways might believing in Santa be the same as believing in God?

5 What did Freud mean by saying that God is a projection of a father-figure?

6 What did Freud mean by saying that God is a projection of our ideal self?

7 In what ways might Freud and Rogers explain why religious experiences are so common throughout time and around the world?

8 Describe what conditions might help someone to "have a religious experience"?

9 What might someone mean if they said that a religious experience was like a placebo effect?

10 In what circumstances might people hallucinate?

11 Do the stories of David Koresh and Jim Jones prove that religious experiences are false? Explain.

12 Does the fact that so many people haven't had a religious experience prove there is no God? Explain.

13 Read Source A again and the comments on it. How does Bowker criticise Freud's theory?

14 Read Source B again and the comments on it. In what way does Russell question the validity of religious experiences?

Practical Activities

1 In your class, get your teacher to play some atmospheric music – something soothing and classical should do it. Each person in the class should close their eyes and listen. Then you should write about what you felt during this. Compare your findings. What common or unusual features were there?

2 Imagine you were to investigate the area of religious experience scientifically. How might you go about it? What information would you want to get? How would you plan to get it? Draw up a plan of action.

3 What is your ideal self? In class each person should write what they think their ideal self would be. This should then be displayed in the class. Similar ideas should be grouped together.

4 On this same board you should add images and stories of people (real or imaginary) who you think are heroes (or examples of what we'd all like to be). This could range from your uncle to superman!

5 Try out the power of suggestion.

Practical Activities continued

i   Ask someone to lift a heavy box for you (which is actually empty)

ii Ask someone to put their hand inside a box where there's a dead mouse (the box is empty)

iii Stand behind someone and tell them you're going to pull them back gently towards you (not let them fall!). Put your hand lightly on their shoulders and then lift your hands off their shoulders (make sure you're still there to catch them!).

iv Mention casually that someone saw a ghost in your school dining canteen. Give it a week and see how many other ghost stories appear.

v   Get people to put their hands together. Now tell them that you are making their hands stick together. When you count to three, people won't be able to get their hands apart. (Remember to tell everyone they can now do this once the experiment is over!)

6 Look back at the previous section. For each of the stories, use what you have learned in this section to explain what really might have been going on.

Unit Assessment Question

Intermediate 1: Outcome 2:
"Religious people say that religious experience is enough proof there's a God" How far is this statement accurate? Give two reasons for your answer.

Intermediate 2: Outcome 3:
"Religious experience can't be verified. Therefore it's not proof that there's a God". To what extent do you agree?

Sample Exam Question

Intermediate 1:
What does a religious person mean when they say they've had a "religious experience"? (4)

Intermediate 2:
"Religious Experiences are just wishful thinking". How far do you agree? (10)

Homework

Look up Sigmund Freud on the internet. Find a quote from Freud's work which shows what he thinks about religion. Explain your views on this quote. Gather these together in your class – they should help you when it comes to assignment/exam time!

Funtime

Look back at the Funtime activity on page 40. Apply the things you have learned in this section to the video, "Homer the Heretic", or to the script which was written for it by people in your class. How could you explain away Homer's "experience"?

Suffering and Evil: The Case Against God

The Potter's Bar Train Crash,
10 May 2002

The Bali bombing,
12 October 2002

Third World Poverty

Why do bad things happen?

There are obviously some things which everyone would agree aren't good – but are they bad? Is there someone or something to blame? Or is it all just part of a natural system where such things are unavoidable?

Task

Discuss: Are there more bad things happening in the world than good?

Suppose you're sitting in a long traffic queue on the first day of your holiday. If you don't get a move on, you'll miss your 'plane. All the money you spent will be lost. The holiday you've looked forward to all year won't happen. You're getting angrier. It's really bad. But hang on, what's causing this? You are. Your car is part of the problem.

Or you're lying in bed, miserable with the cold. Your nose looks like a cartoon nose. Your head is fit to explode. But you picked up this little bug during that nice snog with your girlfriend/boyfriend three days ago – whose fault's that?

Can we really say that these two things are bad? Are they bad in the same way as the events of 11 September 2001? Is dying from cancer the same kind of bad as being murdered? Does everyone agree about what's bad and what isn't? Do bad things happen because of us or something "out there"? What part might a God play in all this – does he take part, or sit back and watch? Or worse still – might he be in some way responsible?

The Fact of Suffering and Evil

Evil and suffering exist. Everyone has experienced something bad – some more serious than others. Evil and suffering force us to ask big questions. Sometimes you might think it's best just to stay indoors and hide from it all – but most accidental deaths happen in the home!

For many people, the fact of the existence of evil and suffering in the world is the most powerful reason for not believing in God – especially a God you can't prove exists. But first, we have to look at the kinds of evil and suffering there are.

Natural Evil: the power of nature

This covers a range of problems. The thing they all have in common is that the suffering they cause is all the result of natural events such as earthquakes, hurricanes, floods and erupting volcanoes. All of these result in loss of life and general misery. They happen all over the world – some in more places than others, and some only in certain places and not others. For example, earthquakes can happen anywhere (yes, even in Scotland!), but the most severe ones happen where the earth's plates meet.

Natural evil

Of course the suffering they cause depends upon them happening where people live. Many strong earthquakes happen in the oceans – causing no real harm, but when even relatively small ones happen where lots of people live, there can be very serious harm caused. This is especially true where the places they happen aren't equipped to cope with them, like the Kobe earthquake in Japan in 1995.

Every moment of every day, there are around 2000 thunderstorms happening on planet earth! In the USA, around 100 people die each year from lightning strikes – but is this figure high or low? The suffering caused by natural evil of this type can be very severe. It is maybe made worse by three important features of natural evil:

◆ Natural evil is random. You suffer if you're at the wrong place at the wrong time

◆ Natural evil is unpredictable. Although you're more likely to die from a volcanic ash cloud if you live near a volcano, you still don't know when it might erupt

◆ Natural evil often causes problems in relation to how well-equipped you are to deal with them. For example, a flood in a poor country will probably cause more harm than one in a rich country.

Natural Evil: the bugs are coming

Natural evil also includes bacteria, viruses, cancer cells and the like. These things are still not properly understood by science. In the case of viruses, they change (mutate) so quickly that no

sooner have you worked out a way to deal with them, than they've changed and you have to start all over again. In Britain, there are more and more cases of what are called superbugs. These are bacteria which have "outsmarted" antibiotics. There could come a time when our antibiotics just don't work because the bacteria have evolved beyond their reach – then we're in trouble.

All over the world, illnesses and diseases – like smallpox and bubonic plague – are making a come-back. All you have to do is cough . . .

Illnesses like cancer aren't understood. Again, things like these are unpredictable and random. Some people live really healthy lives and die young of cancer, whereas others live very unhealthily and live to a ripe old age.

Human Evil

Murders, cruelty, even simple bullying in school can all cause terrible pain and misery. This usually isn't related to where you live or how wealthy you are. You have just as much chance (more?) of being beaten up or murdered in a rich country as a poor one – and you can be bullied in any school, not just a "rough" one. Human evil has many features:

◆ It can be random and unpredictable. In October 2002, a sniper caused mayhem in the USA by – completely randomly – shooting people in the street

◆ There might be no pattern to who is harmed. The Olympic swimmer Ian Thorpe planned to visit the World Trade centre

Task

On a world map, mark the occurrence of natural disasters (state when each one happened and the problems it caused including number of deaths). Do these events prove there's no God?

Human evil

on 11 September 2001, but he went back to his hotel to get his camera first. If he hadn't he'd have been in the building when the 'planes struck it

◆ Human evil can be a deliberate act – and sometimes really strange. Two neighbours in Ratho near Edinburgh didn't get on. Eventually one set fire to the other's house. The woman inside – who was pregnant at the time, died

◆ Human evil can be accidental – the result of a long series of unfortunate consequences. A tired young doctor who gives the wrong medicine to a patient

◆ Human evil can be passive. This means that you don't have to *do* anything. As long as you sit back and do nothing (and let evil happen) you're being bad.

Intention vs Consequences

Human-caused evil obviously causes pain and suffering, but where's the evil in it? Some would say that it's your intention which matters. If you're trying to do bad then that itself is bad – no matter what the outcome is. So suppose I loosen the nuts on the wheels of your car – but you notice before driving away. Is what I've done as bad as it would be if you had driven off and killed yourself? What if someone else saw me doing this and said nothing? How bad is what they have done?

What if your intentions weren't bad, but the consequences were. Suppose you cause a crash and kill someone while over the limit. Even if your intention when driving the car wasn't to

Intentional evil?

kill anyone. Should you be let off with it because you "didn't mean it"? Sometimes the consequences of anyone's actions aren't obvious . . .

You buy banana X instead of Y. This is because banana X is cheaper. This is because less of the money from the sale of banana X goes to the producer. So the producer of banana X isn't getting enough from the sale of his bananas to feed his family. So he grows some drugs on the side to make ends meet. These drugs are bought by international criminals. Their profits come from the untold misery of drug-users. Drug-users who might commit acts of theft and violence to make enough money to feed their habit . . . Now, if only you had bought banana Y instead . . .

Is the international drugs scene partly your fault because you bought banana X?

Could it be you?

People who do bad things might do them because they were born that way, or because they have learned that being bad is the best way to get what they want. Maybe they can't help it because that's how they were brought up. Maybe some people can't help doing bad things. Should some bad actions result in prison and others result in medical treatment? Suppose you were starving. How long would it take before you would get food however you could – even if it meant using violence or stealing it? Should you be blamed for that?

Is that evil?

Task

Think through the things you've bought recently. How could your choices have harmful effects for people? Discuss in class.

Stanley Milgram was a psychologist who wanted to find out if ordinary people would carry out extreme acts of violence. He had been horrified at what people in the concentration camps had done to others during World War II. He wanted to know if there was something wrong with the people who did this – or if anyone would do it given the "right" conditions. He set up a famous experiment. This involved people giving electric "shocks" to other people when they got a question wrong (the shocks weren't real, but the person giving them didn't know that). He found that ordinary people were quite prepared to shock other people to death, provided that they could blame someone else for it. As long as they could say "I was just following orders". According to Milgram, anyone is capable of such extreme acts of violence . . . scary huh?

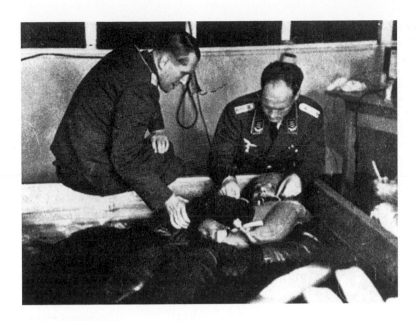

The horrors of Nazi Germany

So is "evil" just survival?

Maybe what we think of as evil is just the survival instinct. It's not good or bad, just nature's way of weeding out the weak or keeping the population regulated. Calling it evil and suffering is just a label we give to it. It doesn't really mean anything. If there weren't viruses and bacteria, then the population would get out of hand – is this just nature's way of keeping humans down? Maybe even human acts of violence and wars for example, are also just nature's way.

Imagine you filled your classroom with 100 people who weren't allowed to leave the room. You'd very quickly find that people got very grumpy with each other. Now suppose they were to stay there for ever! It probably wouldn't be too long before they started to kill each other off to make some room. Is that evil?

There's a wider problem here too – that of *anthropomorphising*. What we think of as evil depends on our point of view. This means that we apply our own, human, ideas of right and wrong, good and bad to places where (maybe) they don't fit. Imagine a cat which has just caught a mouse. It toys with it (tortures it?), and eventually leaves it for dead. It doesn't need to eat it because it gets three tins of cat munchies every day. Should we blame the cat for its evil actions? Should we punish it?

> ## Task
> Do you think animals should be punished for killing each other? Is there any difference between that and human acts of violence?

What about God?

When bad things happen people might ask

Why did God let this happen?

Suffering and Evil – The Case Against God

Anthropomorphising

Now, is this a fair question, or even a sensible question? The next section will try to answer it, but for the moment, let's see what the issue is.

Christians believe that God exists. He has certain qualities:

◆ God is omnipotent: he is all-powerful. There is nothing he can't do if he wants to do it. No one and nothing is stronger than he is

◆ God is omniscient: he is all-knowing. There's nothing he misses, however small

◆ God is perfectly good: there's not a "bad bone in God's body". He is as good as it is possible to be.

Now here's where it might get a little complicated:

A Evil exists. It is a fact.

B If God is all-good then surely he must want to do something about evil. You can't be all good and just sit back and watch bad things happening. If you do, you're just as bad as the people who are doing the bad things.

C But what if he wants to do something but can't. Well, in that case he can't be all powerful. What kind of God would he be then?

D What if he just doesn't notice? Then he can't be all-knowing. Now, you could forgive God for missing your sore knee, but can you really forgive him for failing to notice that guy who is just about to kill the little old lady in her own home?

E What if it's "just nature"? The only problem with that is –

according to Christians – God designed and made everything there is. So is his design a bit off? If God made everything, then he made evil too. This means that he is the cause of evil – or at least partly responsible for it.

F Maybe God just started it all off and then walked away. If so, it means that God isn't interested in our daily lives – so what would be the point in us being interested in him?

'*s not my fault*

Has God lost interest?

G So, many people come to the conclusion that what God is (claimed to be) doesn't match up with the actual existence of evil. So, either Christians have got it wrong and God isn't what they thought he was or Christians have got it wrong entirely because there isn't a God at all.

Source A
www.humanism.org.uk

Apart from the lack of evidence for God, the strongest argument against the existence of God is the whole question of evil and suffering. Many religious people have times when they seriously doubt their faith in God. When they consider horrific events like the murder of the children at Dunblane, they find it difficult to believe in a God who is all-loving and all-powerful. Perhaps God is either not good, or not powerful? But that would go against the teaching of most religions. And if God is cruel, why should people worship? Do they want a cruel God to bring about more cruelty? Perhaps God simply doesn't intervene in human lives? This is like the belief of "Deists", who think that God never reveals himself to us, and so won't intervene to stop bad events. In this case, there is little point in prayer or worship. Perhaps God doesn't care about us? Once again, why worship? Why pray?

Comments

This quote is from the British Humanist Association's Website. The argument is simple. The existence of evil is the most serious challenge to belief in God. The source refers to Deism. This was a view popular in the 19th C which said that God doesn't take part in our day to day activities. Religious people don't think much of Deism, because it means that God's not really interested in us. But, as Humanists point out, if he was interested in us then maybe he should interfere more.

EXISTENCE OF GOD

Source B — http://atheism.about.com

First ... God could have actualised a world with natural laws that made natural disasters less probable. Humans (especially human children) could have been made less vulnerable to various diseases. Countless possibilities are open to an omnipotent being. Second, God need not perform spectacular miracles to help the survivors of natural disasters ... God could perform preventative miracles that He knows will be undetectable by humans. These miracles might include alterations to the positioning of tectonic plates to stop earthquakes, or small modifications in atmospheric conditions to avoid droughts, floods or tornadoes. Third, it is not true that the predictability of nature would be totally broken down in the event of spectacular miracles. It is usually accepted that God intervenes in His world on a frequent basis to perform miracles. God could significantly decrease the quantity of natural evil in the world if He was more efficient in these interventions. For example, instead of performing miracles of apparently little use, such as angelic visitations, Marian manifestations or weeping statues, God could use His limited supply of miracles more efficiently to lessen the harmful effects of natural disasters.

The Evidential Argument from Evil (1998): Nicholas Tattersall

Comments

Tattersall is answering the question of why, if there were a God, he doesn't interfere to stop evil. His argument is that God could do this in a way that we would never have to know he's doing it. He could have made an evil-free world in the first place. Or he could tinker with things to make life a little easier. He argues that the "miracles" many religious people believe he does perform, are pretty pointless when you compare them to what he could be doing to make life more pleasant for all of us.

Activities

Knowledge and Understanding

Intermediate 1

1 Do you think there are some things which are more bad than others? Discuss in your class and note down the views expressed.

2 Describe the last time you did something "bad". Why did you do it?

3 Give two pieces of evidence you could use to prove that evil exists.

4 Here are some examples of evil. Put them into two groups: Natural Evil and Human Evil.

Earthquakes
Hurricanes
Murder
Illness
Bullying
War
Floods
Boredom

5 Match the statements with the explanations
i Natural evil is random
ii Natural evil is unpredictable
iii The effects of natural evil vary
iv Human evil can be deliberate
v Human evil can be accidental
vi Human evil can be passive

Activities continued

a   This means that the consequences weren't thought about.

b   This means you can't predict what might happen.

c   This means bad happens because people let it.

d   This means that the bad things are done on purpose.

e   This means the evil can happen anywhere, anytime.

f   This means that the harm caused might depend on where you live or how poor you are.

6 Is someone not saving someone's life (when they could) as bad as killing them? Explain your answer.

7 Should drink-drivers be charged with murder if they kill someone while driving over the limit? Explain your views.

8 Why might you end up doing evil if you were starving?

9 What did the psychologist Stanley Milgram find?

10 Do you think the question "Why did God let this happen?" is fair?

11 Match up the qualities of God with the explanations
   a   Omniscience
   b   Omnipotence
   c   Perfectly good

   i   This means god is all-powerful – he can do anything
   ii This means God is all-knowing – he knows everything
   iii This means God has no evil in him

12 "God made the universe so he is the cause of all evil". What does this statement mean? Do you agree with it?

13 Why might a religious person not want to believe that God made everything and then just walked away?

14 Read Source A again. This source uses Deism to support its argument. How does it do this?

15 Read Source B again. Give one argument or piece of evidence this source uses to show that God has "failed" in his job as God.

Intermediate 2

1 Give as many examples as you can which prove that evil exists.

2 In what way is the existence of evil a challenge for religious people?

3 Give three examples of natural evil. What are their causes?

4 Explain how the effects of natural evil aren't always he same.

5 Do you agree that natural evil is random? Explain your answer.

6 What does it mean to say that natural evil is unpredictable?

7 In what ways might human actions be "helping" natural evil? (clue: "bugs")

8 In what ways could human evil be accidental?

9 What does it mean to say that human evil can be passive?

10 In your opinion, is it worse to kill someone or to let them die? Explain your answer.

11 When thinking about human evil, what's more important, the intention or the consequences? Explain.

12 In what ways might you be to blame for the violent acts of a drug user?

13 Describe the work of Stanley Milgram. Has he proved that everyone is capable of evil?

14 What might it mean to say that evil doesn't exist – it's just nature's way? What do you think?

Activities continued

15 Is weeding your garden an act of evil?

16 In your own words, describe the three qualities of God which most religious people believe he has.

17 Now explain in what ways these qualities might be questioned by the existence of evil.

18 How might someone argue that God is the cause of all evil?

19 Read Source A again. How does the writer use Deism to support his argument?

20 Read Source B again. How does this writer challenge the existence of God?

Practical Activities

1 Design and make a collage of images for display in your classroom which shows the existence of evil in the world today. Try to mix a variety of things from global issues to more local ones. You shouldn't find this hard because newspapers seem to like stories about bad things!

2 On a different display board get everyone in your class to (anonymously!) write down something bad that they once did. These could be written on small pieces of card – or better still typed up individually.

3 A recent anti-litter campaign highlighted the fact that more litter = more rats and more rats = more possibility for disease. Design a poster which alerts people to one of the following;
   - Litter causes rats causes disease
   - Mis-using antibiotics allows superbugs to develop
   - Bad hygiene causes ill health
   - Unhealthy lifestyle might lead to early death

   - Alcohol can lead to violence
   - Travel abroad spreads disease

4 Have a class debate: "Something is bad only if it has bad consequences".

5 Find out more about the work of Stanley Milgram and the activities of concentration camp guards which made him want to know why they did what they did. Write a brief report of your findings. Are all humans potential killers?

6 Some animal rights activists believe that people should be prosecuted for killing animals (whether for food or anything else). One answer to this would be that animals too would then have to be prosecuted for the same thing. Set up a court case in your class where a cat is accused of murdering a mouse. Work out the prosecution and defence arguments and try the case.

Unit Assessment Question

Intermediate 1: Outcome 3:
Does the existence of Evil challenge belief in God? Give two reasons for your answer

Intermediate 2: Outcome 1:
In what ways is the existence of evil a problem for religious believers?

Sample Exam Question

Intermediate 1:
How might someone argue that the existence of evil proves there is no God? (4)

Intermediate 2:
"The problem of evil is the strongest argument against the existence of God" To what extent do you agree? (10)

Homework

Some people would argue that the only reason we think the world is full of evil, is because that's all we hear about in the news. Choose one newspaper. Count the number of articles in it about bad things in the world and compare this with the number about good things. Why do you think there are more stories about bad things?

Funtime

Write a letter to God: "Why do you allow suffering". Pass it to someone in your class. Get them to write "God's reply".

Suffering and Evil: The Case For God

I am not skilled to understand
What God hath willed, what God hath planned;
I only know at his right hand
Stands One who is my Saviour

I take God at his word and deed:
Christ died to save me, this I read;
And in my heart I find a need
Of Him to be my Saviour

And was there then no other way
For God to take? I cannot say;
I only bless him day by day,
Who saved me through my Saviour.

Dora Greenwell (1821–82) (Methodist Publishing
House 1933 Hymn 381)

RMPS ... and Faith

Many religious people won't give the things you're having to
study a second thought (they're not trying to pass an exam in

RMPS – concentrate!

RMPS, you are!). Their answer to the problem of evil is one based on faith. The hymn opposite gives you an idea of this. Evil exists – no one can deny it, but there's no point in trying to understand it. We can't understand why God allows bad things to happen – we have to get on with our lives and believe. Maybe we'll get the answers later. But as far as your studies are concerned …

Task

Discuss: What do you think are the advantages and disadvantages of studying RMPS in school?

Changing God's qualities

One way to try to deal with the problem of evil through argument is to forget about the qualities usually linked to God. This gives us a way out of the problem of evil, but reduces God to an under-achiever. So, let's say God isn't omniscient, omnipotent or perfectly good. Almost all Christians would reject this approach to the problem, but not all religions have.

Some religions see the universe as a constant struggle between the forces of good and the forces of evil – finely balanced. Some have suggested that God has many natures. In Hinduism for example, God is seen as Creator, Preserver and Destroyer all in one. Some faiths believe that God is both good and evil (Dualism). Others think God is good, but still has to battle with evil all the time. Christians have always avoided these kinds of views. For them, God is omnipotent, omniscient and perfectly good.

All things to all people?

Evil isn't real

Some religions have argued that calling something evil is just a way of looking at things. For example, take a cancer cell. Is it evil? It's just a collection of atoms arranged in a particular way. It certainly causes pain and suffering. But working out at the gym can also cause pain and suffering. We are prepared to accept one form of suffering, but not another. In fact we call one evil and the other pleasure. Humans demonstrate some funny (contradictory?) ideas.

Many Eastern religions, such as Buddhism, have taken this view. Evil is an illusion – no more no less, but then so is good. Some Christians agree. They have argued that God can be found in suffering just as much as he can be found in joy. If all creation is God's work, then a cancer cell is just as much God's creation as a flower. It is our choice to call one beautiful and the other ugly. If evil doesn't exist, then there's no problem of evil and there's no threat to belief in God.

> **Task**
>
> Have a class debate: "Evil isn't real".

Evil isn't real

The Devil

Many religious people will argue that evil is the work of the Devil. This partly reduces the problem of evil – when bad things happen, that's who to blame. The trouble with this view is that it doesn't fit with the qualities of God.

If God's omnipotent, he should be able to control the Devil. The Devil sometimes getting the better of God doesn't fit with what religious people believe God is. God shouldn't allow the Devil to do evil – because then God would be just as bad as the Devil.

God created the Devil

Besides, according to Christians, God made the angels – one of whom became the Devil by falling out with God. Didn't God know this was going to happen? Shouldn't God have ended the Devil's existence right away – or at least when it became obvious that the Devil was going to be an almighty nuisance?

Once we suggest that the Devil is the cause of all evil, we don't actually help God out very much at all. It can be argued too easily that the Devil is God's work! Even if we argue that in some way God and the Devil are "evenly matched" this takes us into Dualism, which for Christians is a very weak defence of God.

Task

Discuss: Do you think there's a Devil?

The Free Will argument

The Free Will argument was first used by St Augustine as a way to explain the existence of evil. For many Christians it is the most obvious argument to explain why God does appear to allow bad things to happen.

The argument goes like this:

◆ God made humans →

◆ He gave them freedom to choose, good or bad →

◆ When humans choose bad, God doesn't interfere →

◆ Otherwise humans would not be free at all – we'd be God's puppets →

◆ The freedom to choose is the most important thing →

◆ The fact that evil sometimes comes out of our choices can't be helped.

Free Will

For many Christians, this is argument enough. Human evil is the result of human choices. You can't blame anyone but yourself for your choices. Even when the effects (on you) were caused by someone else's choices you still can't complain. Freedom to choose has to apply to everyone equally or not at all, otherwise this would be unfair and make the whole business of allowing human freedom silly. If this is true then God is unhappy every time someone chooses to do evil – but he doesn't do anything about it because then he would be taking away human freedom.

Christians believe that the Fall is the first example of this. God creates Adam and Eve and gives them the freedom to choose. They choose to disobey God and so God punishes them. But

God gave us the ability to choose

their action has now brought evil into the world. Possible criticisms of this argument might be:

◆ Why is freedom to choose more valuable than anything else? Is the death of a child murdered by an adult of less value than the adult's right to make the free choice to kill the child?

◆ Couldn't God always make us choose the right thing without us noticing? Religious people argue that he couldn't because then our freedom would only be an illusion. But wouldn't that be worth it to live in a world which is free of evil?

◆ How can the free choices exercised by Adam and Eve lead to the evil caused by nature in the form of earthquakes for example?

◆ Why did God give Adam and Eve freedom and then punish them because they didn't choose what God wanted them to? You either give someone freedom or you don't.

For many religious people, this is the bottom line argument for the existence of human evil. If you're not free to choose evil, then you're not free to choose good either.

Task

In your own words, explain what religious people mean by the Free Will argument. What do you think of it?

Natural Evil

Volcanoes don't have choices, so the Free Will argument can't work here. Religious people have explained this kind of evil in this way:

◆ God made a universe

◆ This universe is based on the unchangeable laws of physics

◆ This means that natural events follow patterns of cause and effect which can't be changed

Physics can't be controlled

◆ Sometimes this results in bad things happening

◆ God cannot interfere and break the laws he himself made

◆ If the laws of physics were fiddled about with by God – sometimes and not others – then we'd never be sure about anything.

Logically contradictory

For example, imagine God dampened down a tornado as it approached a town. People saw this happen. Before long you'd have people rushing towards tornadoes, knowing that God would put it out at just the right moment. Now God would have to dampen every tornado ... and plug every volcano, settle every earthquake ... The world we live in would become a completely crazy place. You could pick up a gun and shoot someone ... God would stop the bullet ... and so on. Maybe God can't do things which make no sense. This doesn't threaten his omnipotence, because it's just too loopy to think about. It is what philosophers call *logically contradictory*. For example:

1 God's Omnipotence allows him to create anything

2 He can therefore create a tomato of any size and weight

3 He can therefore create a tomato which is so heavy he can't lift it

4 He must therefore be able to create something which defeats his own omnipotence!

CS Lewis argued that it is not a limit on God's omnipotence to say that he can't do completely contradictory things. But some have argued that God could sometimes stop bad things happening and not others without making everything crazy. Maybe he could let earthquakes happen where no people lived, but stop ones which could harm large cities so they didn't kill anyone. We'd never know about it, and the laws of physics – as far as we were concerned – wouldn't have changed at all.

Necessary Evil

Some have the view that evil is *logically necessary.* This means that if you didn't have evil, then you would never know what good was. Earthquakes have to happen – or we wouldn't know how lucky we are when they don't. In short, you can't have a top without a bottom. So, there has to be contrast. If everything in the world was perfectly good, then we'd never know it – because we'd have nothing to compare it to. So if you take away sadness, you'd have to take away joy too.

Task

Explain in your own words what someone might mean by saying that evil is "necessary". What do you think of the argument?

Free Choice and Natural Evil

Some religious people have argued that the pain and suffering caused by natural evil could be avoided by using our free choices, exercising our God-given brain. Tokyo has a population of around 13 million. Yet it is built on one of the most seismically active areas in the world. There might be a very close link between smoking and cancer yet people still choose to smoke. There seems to be almost no incidence of cancer in native peoples like the Yanomami of Brazil, yet in the developed world it is a major killer. What's going on? Is this our lifestyle choices making the effects of natural evil worse? Maybe we shouldn't complain about volcanoes erupting when we choose to live on their slopes!

Using your brain?

Suffering and Evil – The Case For God

God's Use of Evil

Evil as a Punishment? In the past it was widely believed by Christians that God used pain and suffering as a punishment. It was a way to bring people back to him – even if it was a bit of an extreme method. This view is not very popular with most religious people today. But might God use evil?

Good comes out of Evil? Some Christians argue that God uses evil for greater good. Sometimes it's the best (or only?) way to bring about some good outcome. Every major tragic event seems to bring out the best in people. Many religious people believe that there is great value in suffering – and that life would be less rewarding without it. Of course, people who oppose this view would say that there surely must be a better way. Why should some people suffer and die so that others learn things?

Evil is part of God's Plan? Some religious people argue that the point of suffering is beyond our understanding. It is all part of what they call "God's Plan". We can't know why it is happening, because God alone knows. What we have to do is trust that God knows what he is doing, and so whatever is happening to us is for some reason.

Task
Discuss: Do you think a God could be responsible for evil?

Evil and Proof of God

The existence of evil does present many challenges to the belief that God exists. But it does not prove that there is no God. Maybe it challenges what we think God is or should be, but it can't be as simple as saying that evil exists and therefore God doesn't. One doesn't automatically follow from the other.

Evil is part of the plan

Source A

Can a world in which sadistic cruelty often has its way, in which selfish lovelessness is so rife, in which there are debilitating diseases, crippling accidents, bodily and mental decay, insanity and all manner of natural disasters be regarded as the expression of infinite creative goodness? Certainly all this could never by itself lead anyone to believe in the existence of a limitlessly powerful God. And yet even in a world which contains these things innumerable men and women have believed and do believe in the reality of an infinite creative goodness, which they call God …

Encountering Evil – John Hick *Live Options in Theodicy* (S Davies (Ed) p 39)

Comments

John Hick is saying here that faith can be just as strongly supported in bad times as in good. His argument here is that if you live with God in your life … somehow, the problem of evil is something you can live with. Hick also wrote a very famous book called 'Evil and the God of Love'. In this he defends what he calls the Irenaean Theodicy. This argument is that humans had to have freedom so that they could "evolve" into a proper relationship with God. Along the way, this would mean bad choices, but that is part of the process. Evil is necessary because it is a stage on the way to humans becoming what God wants them to be. In other words, the ends justify the means.

Source B

If men are to have knowledge of the evil which will result from their actions or negligence, laws of nature must operate regularly; and that means there will be what I may call, 'victims of the system' … if men are to have the opportunity to bring about serious evils for themselves or others by actions or negligence, or to prevent their occurrence, and if all knowledge of the future is obtained by normal … induction from patterns of similar events in the past – then there must be serious natural evils occurring to man …

The Existence of God – Richard Swinburne (Oxford 1979 p 210)

Comments

Swinburne's argument is that evil is necessary, because otherwise humans aren't truly free. The only way we can really learn what's good and what's bad is by trial and error – by exercising our free choices. If, when we chose to do bad, God stepped in and stopped us, then we would never know what the outcome of our action would have been – so we'd never learn from it. So actual evil has to happen if we choose to do it. Anything else would be a restriction on our freedom to choose.

◆ Many people choose to live on the slopes of Mount Vesuvius in Italy – even though they know that it will erupt at some point

◆ It is estimated that there are between 300 and 500 chemicals in our bodies which wouldn't have been there 50 years ago. These come from things we *choose* to have. Maybe one of them is the cause of cancer

◆ Despite being aware of the risks, most people still choose to use cars. It is estimated that around 500,000 people die in traffic accidents around the world every year (source: Red Cross).

Facts and Figures

Activities

Knowledge and Understanding

Intermediate 1

1 Why might many religious people not bother with the things you're having to study?

2 Copy and complete these two sentences matching the right endings to the right beginnings:

a   If we ignore the ideas of omniscience, omnipotence and perfectly good then . . .

b   But if we do this then . . .

i   we make God into an under-achiever and he's no longer the kind of God most religious people would want to believe in.

ii   we can ignore the problem of evil because it's not in God's control.

3 Which religion thinks of God as creator, preserver and destroyer?

4 What is meant by Dualism?

5 Copy the correct statements from the list below:

i   Buddhism teaches that evil is an illusion

ii   Buddhism teaches that evil is real

iii   A cancer cell is the work of the Devil

iv   A cancer cell is part of God's creation

v   God can be found in suffering

vi   God can only be found in happiness

vii   What's bad depends on your point of view

viii   Suffering is always suffering

6 How might a religious person use the Devil to explain away evil?

7 Give one reason why God could be blamed for the work of the Devil.

8 From the list below, order the statements into two groups:

a   Advantages of the Free Will argument

b   Disadvantages of the Free Will argument

i   It makes evil our own fault

ii   It makes God seem kind in giving us total freedom

iii   It takes away the responsibility for evil from God

iv   It doesn't explain why God couldn't stop evil without us knowing

v   Why is freedom the most important thing?

vi   Why should other people suffer so that I have free choice?

vii   It doesn't explain natural evil

9 Could God create a tomato he couldn't lift? Explain your answer.

10 Switch the underlined words with * in this paragraph so that they make sense;

Activities continued

Some <u>good</u> people believe that * has to exist. If evil didn't exist then we would never <u>evil</u> know what * was. If you take away, * <u>necessary</u> you have to take away joy. So, evil is logically * <u>sadness</u>.

11 Why might people living in California be a good reason for not blaming God for natural evil?

12 Would most religious people agree nowadays that God uses evil to punish people?

13 Here are some statements which have appeared in this section. For each one explain what it means and say whether you agree with it or not.

   i   Good can come out of evil.
   ii   Evil is part of God's plan.
   iii Evil is logically necessary.
   iv Evil happens because of our free choices.
   v   Evil happens because the laws of nature have to stay the same, wherever, whenever.
   vi What is evil depends on your point of view.

14 Do you think the existence of evil proves there's no God? Explain your answer.

15 Read Source A again. Does John Hick believe that you can only have faith when things are going well?

16 Read Source B again. Copy any part of this quote which shows that it is an example of the Free Will argument.

Intermediate 2

1 What do you think of the approach to religion which is suggested by Dora Greenwell's Hymn?

2 What do you think is helpful/unhelpful about your studies in RMPS?

3 In you opinion, is ignoring the qualities of omniscience, omnipotence and perfect goodness a good way to deal with the problem of evil? Explain your answer.

4 Do you think evil is real? Explain your answer.

5 How might the Devil be a way out of the problem of evil for Christians?

6 What problems are there with using the Devil in this way?

7 Why don't Christians think much of Dualism?

8 In your own words, explain what is meant by the Free Will argument.

9 Do you think the Free Will argument solves the problem of evil? Explain your answer.

10 Why might a religious person argue that natural evil *has* to happen?

11 What is meant by *logically contradictory*?

12 Do you think some evil (or all evil) is necessary? Explain.

13 What part might human choice play in natural evil?

14 Why would a Christian today not like the idea that God might use suffering as a punishment?

15 What might someone mean by saying that good can come out of evil and suffering? Do you agree?

16 What does it mean to say that evil is "part of God's plan"? Do you think this is a helpful argument?

17 In your opinion, does the problem of evil prove there is no God? Explain your answer.

18 Read Source A again. In your own words, explain Hick's argument.

19 Read Source B again. How does Swinburne justify the existence of evil?

EXISTENCE OF GOD

Practical Activities

1 With your teacher's help find some more Bible stories which seem to go against the idea that God is Omniscient, Omnipotent and Perfectly Good. Write a report about each story and how it goes against the particular belief. How do religious people try to explain it.

2 Design a display board on "God and the Devil". Show the features usually given to each of them. How are they "linked"? You'll have to do some further research for this one.

3 If this is not possible, write a short script for a one-act play, where God and the Devil meet up. Here God blames the Devil for all bad things and the Devil argues back.

4 Here is a letter written in a newspaper following some tragic event. Write a response to it which could be made by a religious person.

Dear Sir,

As I was walking along Argyle Street yesterday I heard them again. The holy rollers shouting at me that I was a sinner and God is love. Then I go home and turn on the news. Suicide bombers, the needless death of children, wars, poverty – the odd earthquake or two. And through all this I'm supposed to believe in a God of love, who cares for everyone. Come on, isn't it time to state the obvious. Why doesn't he just make the bad people disappear? Who'd miss them? Why doesn't he just ease up those tectonic plates. The answer is simple – he doesn't because he can't, and he can't because he doesn't exist. So, holy rollers – away home and take up a useful hobby.

Yours sincerely

Fed-up-listening-to-them of Drumry.

5 Imagine God did step in and stop every bad action. Write a short imaginative story about what a day in your life could be like.

6 Prepare a graffiti board for your class on the problem of evil. Everyone in the class should write their own views on this topic and put them up for display.

Unit Assessment Question

Intermediate 1: Outcome 3:
Do you think that religious responses to the problem of evil work? Give at least two reasons for your answer.

Intermediate 2: Outcome 2:
Christians have been unsuccessful in dealing with the challenges of the problem of evil. How far do you agree?

Sample Exam Question

Intermediate 1:
How might a Christian explain the problem of evil? (4)

Intermediate 2:
"Evil is necessary so that good may come out of it". How far do you agree? (6)

Homework

Take one of the responses to the letter in Practical Activity 4 above. Now write a response to that, showing how you don't accept that it deals with the problem of evil.

Funtime

Have a court trial in your class. The accused is God. The charge is allowing bad things to happen. Think up your prosecution and defence arguments and try the case. Have an objective jury to make the decision based on the evidence they hear – not their already existing prejudices one way or the other!

The Scientific Method

Daydreaming in his RMPS class one day, Liam feels he's being watched. He looks around. Lesley, the pretty new girl in his class, smiles at him. Could it be that she fancies him? Surely not? He looks around at the others in the class. She's not smiling at any of them. Maybe it's just a nervous twitch. He asks Gus (agreed to be the ugliest looking boy in the class) to smile at Lesley whenever she seems to catch his eye. He does. Lesley scrunches her face up in disgust – or maybe she's got wind. So Liam tries the same approach with Chris (who *all* the girls fancy). But there's no reaction from Lesley. So next time she smiles at Liam, he smiles back – bigtime. Lesley blushes and looks down at her work . . . But she's still smiling. It can only mean . . . she does fancy Liam. Now it's his turn to make a move . . . (gulp).

Only **H**amsters **E**at **V**omit

What Liam has just done is called the scientific method.

Observation – He noticed Lesley smiling at him

Hypothesis – He came up with a possible theory about what might be happening – that she fancies him

Experiment – He tried out a few things to test his hypothesis – he asked Gus to see if she would smile at him

Verification – The findings of his experiment lead to him reaching the conclusion that his hypothesis was true (lucky him)

In an everyday situation, this is science in action. That's all science is – a formal system of trial and error. Add in the scientific knowledge gained by those who have gone before you and you have it – science. This case also illustrates the chance observation of something which you'd like to find the answer to. The history of science is full of situations where people saw something fairly ordinary and then asked the question, "why did that happen?".

Task

Apply this method to the following question – Are blondes stupid?

Blonde experiment

The Details

Observation – We see things around us all the time. Science begins when we ask questions about what we see. For example, why do things fall down and not up? It could also be that we observe something unusual – which only happens at certain times of day or following certain other actions.

Hypothesis – This is basically an educated guess. Following our observations, we suggest what could be the cause of what we see. We predict that the cause might be X. Then we test if X is the cause, or if it is something else entirely (or something like X).

Experiment – This is a controlled examination of the evidence – putting it to the test to see whether X causes Y. You need to make sure that this is what you are testing so the whole thing has to be very carefully controlled so that other influences which could spoil your experiment (variables) are kept to a minimum. You have to be completely honest and objective when you do your experiment. Even if this means that your hypothesis is shown to be wrong.

Verification – Your report is used by others so that they can do the same thing and verify (or replicate) your findings. By following your description of your experiment, they should be able to do it exactly the same way, and get exactly the same results. If they can't then maybe you did something wrong in your experiment (on purpose or by accident). If the same thing is found over and over again, then it becomes a scientific principle.

Task

Do you think everything can be proved by science?

Scientific Proof

A proper understanding of science says that things are never proved, only supported. In fact, all you can really say is that the hypothesis is supported. This means that the "proof" is only as good as the last experiment's results. Scientists know that some unknown piece of evidence might still be out there which could challenge what has been "proved" at any time. Once new evidence is found, scientists should be ready to chuck the old theory away and try out a new one.

Is that a fact?

"This is a scientific fact" is a brave statement to make – because the "fact" is only the result of particular experiments understood in particular ways, and based on the evidence gained from the experiment(s).

In daily life you'd get pretty muddled if you started to think this way. Is gravity a fact? You'd soon discover if you tried to test it by leaping off a 12 foot high wall. For everyday discussion things seem proved and seem to be facts – but in strict scientific discussion, the use of such phrases has to be done carefully.

Really important scientific things

Deduction: This means that if X applies then Y follows. Scientists don't have to see everything happen, or to try every possibility. They can work out that if something is the case in a

Gravity is a fact

SCIENCE AND BELIEF

particular situation, then it will almost certainly be the case in a similar situation. This is often referred to as the (wait for it) hypothetico-deductive method.

Light is a perfect example – you can't "see" light waves you can only "see" them when they light something up! So you deduce that there is some force causing what you experience. The only trouble with this is that sometimes it doesn't seem to work as easily as others. For example: atoms are invisible → gorillas are made of atoms → therefore gorillas are invisible (?)

Peek-a-boo!

An invisible gorilla

Reduction: Science reduces things to the bits that make up the whole thing. A human can be reduced to the chemicals that make us up – but does that then mean we are just a collection of chemicals?

Inference: Science begins by learning facts about particular things, and then it applies them more generally (extrapolation). This means that evidence in a particular case can be widened out to apply to all similar (or closely similar) examples. This also means that you can infer a rule always applying when you have seen it apply many times already. Again you have to be cautious about what you do here. Suppose you have only ever

A model of a chemical compound

SCIENCE AND BELIEF

seen pink hippos. Can you then say that this proves there's no such thing as a green hippo?

Verifiability and Falsifiability: To be a scientific question, something has to be able to be verified (able to be shown to be right) or able to be falsified (able to be shown to be wrong). If it's not, then it's outside the area we call science. For example, this is (probably!) not a valid scientific question: "Is the planet furthest from the Earth (in the universe) made of custard?". This statement is not verifiable or falsifiable. You can't prove it or disprove it because we can't get there to find out (yet). So, this question isn't a suitable area of study for science. In fact, it's a question science can't answer.

Models: Science often uses models to explain complex ideas. These are helpful ways of allowing us to imagine things which we otherwise can't get a picture of in our heads. For example, chemicals are often modelled using different coloured straws and wee plastic thingies. This helps us visualise the real thing. But of course, the models are only models, not the real thing.

How do we know?

Flip a coin. It'll land heads or tails up. It's a 50/50 thing. Now decide that you're going to flip it 100 times. You flip it 99 times and each time it lands heads up. Which side will it land up the 100th time?

Lots of people fall right into the trap of saying "heads up". This is because they think that if it has fallen heads up 99 times it's got more chance of doing the same again on the 100th attempt

In fact, it still has a 50/50 chance of landing either heads up or tails up (unless there's some property of the coin we don't know about yet).

In the same way, which set of 6 numbers has most chance of winning the Lottery?

4, 10, 18, 26, 35, 42 OR 1, 2, 3, 4, 5, 6?

Feelings?

Everything said so far makes science out to be what we sometimes think it is anyway – cool, detached, logical, reasonable – no emotions here then. Or are there?

Scientists have feelings

Science is supposed to be *objective* (and so are scientists). This means that you study the problem and come up with the answers – whatever they are. If they prove your hypothesis wrong, then that's fine. You just hold your head high and get slapped on the back for being so brave. It might mean that your life's work has just gone down the pan, but never mind – you aren't involved in your work so you won't be upset … Aye right.

Scientists are human. As humans, when we think we're right we stick with it – even when everything goes against us. It's probably just as well – lots of great scientific discoveries depended on the scientists sticking with their theories even when things seemed to be going against them (of course, you only ever hear about the ones that got it right … eventually!). But science is sometimes quite personal. What we think of as cold, hard facts, are sometimes more emotionally loaded than they seem. In the same way, scientists should be interested in evidence which is a bit "out of place".

Blank minds?

Scientists don't have them! Science is done at particular times and places and scientists bring their own ideas and understandings of the way the world is to work. This can affect how they interpret what they find during their scientific enquiries. Sometimes this is obvious, other times not so.

> ### Task
> Do you think science can be abused? How might this happen? Can you find any examples of this in daily life?

You read a scientific report by a Professor Ffordyce-McSporran (a top man in his scientific field) which says that cigarettes are good for you. Good grief, you think – doesn't that seem a bit odd? That goes against everything else you've ever learned about ciggies. But there it is, with all the maths to prove it and everything. But then you read on. It seems that the good Professor's research was funded by the Tobacco Grower's Association of Baffin Island. They paid his wages during his research. They even bought him a nice new laboratory to do the work in . . .

Are you still so sure about the Professor's findings? Science has to be paid for, and scientists need to keep their wagemasters happy! Of course, sometimes it's not as nasty as the Ffordyce-McSporran example, but sometimes its hard to avoid. Might a scientist working for Greenpeace come up with some research which says that drilling for oil's a really good thing?

Professor Ffordyce-McSporran

There's also the wee problem of just how much the experiment (and experimenter) affects the outcome of the experiment. Maybe as soon as you put something to the test you change the way it is. So, the reactions you get depend – partly anyway – on you and what you're doing.

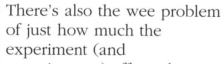

Task

Imagine you had to interview the professor about his findings. What questions would you ask him?

How far can science go?

When an art-lover looks at a beautiful painting it can produce powerful emotions – awe, amazement, beauty, insignificance . . . But what is the painting? Nothing but coloured chemicals on materials stretched around a wooden frame. The paints are probably synthetically produced in a factory. But then they are used by the artist to conjure up something quite incredible – can science explain this? Maybe partly.

Your feelings are, after all, simply neural impulses following a particular pattern from your dendrites to your axons . . . along the billions of neurons you have to specific locations in your brain. But does this really explain the power of the painting?

Probably not. It's a fair bet that there are some things that science just can't get into.

Is love explainable scientifically, or poetry? Good scientists know the boundaries of what they can (and can't) do. Science is a useful tool for explaining all kinds of different things – but maybe we shouldn't expect it to be able to do everything. "What is love?" isn't a question which can be answered by the scientific method.

Science can tell us how things work but it can't give us much guidance about what to do with that knowledge. For example, you can look up the internet and find out how to build a nuclear bomb – all the science is there. But there's no scientific way of working out whether you should use it or not. "Is it right to use a nuclear bomb?" This isn't a question which can be answered by the scientific method. Science can tell us what we *can* do – but not what we *should* do.

Also, science can't come up with the answers to "ultimate questions". It can tell us how human life began and developed – but it can't tell us why humans exist. It can't tell us what life's meaning is. For these reasons some have said that science can answer the "How?" questions, but not the "Why?" questions. This is probably a bit too simplistic but it does point us in the right direction.

> ### Task
> Discuss: What questions can science probably not answer?

Science and Religion – stick to your home ground?

Science and religion have been friends, enemies – and sometimes just haven't spoken to each other much. They've had huge bust-ups and lots of niggly wee arguments. But ... the idea that science and religion are opposites is a fairly old-fashioned one. They are two ways of exploring the mysteries of the universe – each has its own way of doing it – but that's not to say that one is always better than the other. They're both good at different things. It's only once they start to cross over into each other's territory that things can get a little heated.

It definitely wasn't always that way – and there have been mistakes on both sides. For example, many early scientists had a hard time of it from the Christian Church because it seemed that the things they were discovering went against Christian teaching. In fact, what they were usually going against was the Christian Church – and the powerful people who ran it! On the other hand, many of the first scientists were religious people. Gregor Mendel, the father of genetics, was a Christian monk.

SCIENCE AND BELIEF

Science and religion don't always mix

The bottom line is that if you try to get science to answer religious questions – or religion to answer scientific ones – then things are probably going to get messy.

Source A

What has been the most widely accepted view of science in recent years – includes a view of the scientific attitude. It is the view of the scientist as a man who (ideally) never supposes that he has reached finality, never supposes that he has reached the final truth. For one thing, if there were such a thing as the final truth, how could anyone know that he had attained it? . . . Scientists work on their own and other scientists' theories, and never rest in the belief that no better theories can be obtained than [exist at the moment]. . . . Also;

1 Scientists generalise.
2 The scientist's methods are empirical . . . about things . . . open to sense inspection.
3 Scientists use models . . . as a way of reducing . . . abstract thought to a graspable form.
4 In many sciences, mathematics is an indispensable tool . . .

T McPherson *Philosophy & Religious Belief* (Hutchinson University Library: London 1974. pp 108–110)

Comments

The writer points out that science is a something you do, not just something you find out. It is an ongoing thing. Good scientists should always be on the lookout to improve their theories and challenge the theories of others. Scientists also use specific methods which are different to religion. This means that they are likely to come up with different results. You couldn't answer the question "Is there a God" by coming up with a mathematical formula (not as far as we know yet anyway!).

Source B

Perhaps you find it hard to accept that Jesus could rise from the dead because you have never known anyone rise from the dead. The way it is sometimes expressed is "No-one rises from the dead. Therefore Jesus couldn't have, it's impossible".

That is actually a very unscientific approach. Here we have a theory (that no one can rise from the dead) and a claimed observation that conflicts with it (that Jesus rose from the dead). Now, the good scientist won't disregard the observation because it doesn't fit the theory. No, the good scientist will investigate the observation as much as he can, and if it holds up he will modify his theory . . .

6th Dimension Aerobics for Brain Cells from Scripture Union: www. Homepages.tcp.co.uk/ carling/6thdim2.html

Comments

This shows that good scientists follow things up which don't match the starting theory – because these could provide the answer which is true. This article goes on to mention that Galileo's observations about the "movement" of the sun round the earth seemed to suggest that the earth moved round the sun – but this went against the accepted theory of the day. Science should be about open minds – but the article seems to suggest that scientists don't often have very open minds about religion – because a lot of what they find there goes against today's accepted theories.

- ◆ Galileo Galilei (1564–1642) discovered that the Earth moved round the sun. The Roman Catholic Church officially said that he was right . . . in the year 2000

- ◆ Einstein famously said; "Science without religion is lame, religion without science is blind"

- ◆ Hundreds of reports about new scientific findings are published *every week*

Facts and Figures

Activities

Knowledge and Understanding

Intermediate 1

1 This is the scientific method. Put the parts in the right order:

> **Experiment**   **Observation**
> **Verification**   **Hypothesis**

2 In the Liam and Lesley story, describe Liam's "experiments".

3 Think of three everyday things you observe which might make you ask "Why does that happen?".

4 Match the words with the right explanations:

> **variables**   **hypothesis**
> **verification**   **results**

Explanations:

i   an educated guess about a cause of something

ii   when something is supported or shown to be right

iii   things which can influence your experiment one way or another iv. your findings

5 True/False quiz. Copy the sentences which are right. Find the correct answer for the ones which are wrong. (Some you might need to talk through!)

- Deduction means that if X applies, Y follows
- Reduction means putting things together to make sense of them
- Extrapolation means taking what you know about a particular thing and applying it generally
- If no one's ever seen a green hippo that means green hippos don't exist
- Verifiable means that something can be shown to be right
- Falsifiable means the same as verifiable

- Scientists use supermodels to explain complex ideas
- Scientists don't let their feelings get in the way of their work

6 What should a (good) scientist do when he finds out something which goes against the theory he's investigating?

7 What do you think of the findings of Professor Ffordyce-McSporran? Expain your answer.

8 Which of these questions are things you think can't be investigated by science?

- What is love?
- What happens after I die?
- How does a nuclear bomb work?
- Should we clone people?
- What is life for?
- What is a heart?
- Does the earth go round the sun?

9 "Science and religion should stick to their home ground". What does this mean?

10 Read Source A Comments again. What should "good scientists" always be on the lookout to do?

11 Read Source B again. According to this source, why might someone not believe that Jesus rose from the dead?

Intermediate 2

1 In your own words, describe what is meant by the scientific method.

2 How might an observation lead to a hypothesis?

3 Why would a scientist want to find out about the work of other scientists (into the same area of study) before designing his own experiment?

Activities continued

4 Why do scientists write reports after their experiments? (Think of as many reasons as you can.)

5 Why are scientists cautious about saying that they have "proved" something?

6 Why do many scientists not like the idea of reduction?

7 Do you think that the numbers 1, 2, 3, 4, 5, 6 are ever likely to come up a lottery winning numbers? Explain your answer.

8 "All swans have white or black feathers". Explain whether this is a verifiable/falsifiable statement or not.

9 When might scientists not be as objective as they should?

10 Why shouldn't we expect science to answer everything?

11 Do science and religion have to be opposites? Explain your answer.

12 Read Source A again. How does this describe the ideal scientist?

13 Read Source B again. When should a scientist modify his theory?

Practical Activities

1 Using the following examples, design experiments to test the hypotheses; (you should write these out)

   • Chocolate custard goes off more quickly than yellow custard
   • Blondes are less intelligent that brunettes
   • Pets recognise their owners
   • Eating cheese late at night gives you nightmares

2 Try one of these experiments out. Now write up a report of what you have done in a way which another "scientist" could follow so that they could verify/falsify your results.

3 Use the flip a coin/lottery numbers example to carry out a survey – how many people "fall into the trap"? How many "see through it"?

4 Make a model of DNA (this'll be helpful for the section on the origin of life).

5 Search using the Internet to see if you can find an example of an issue where scientists disagree. Write about your findings. Is the disagreement completely objective? (Hint – environmental issues and genetic engineering might be two areas where you'll find scientific disagreement.)

6 Make your own lists of "Questions science can answer" and "Questions science can't answer". Do this in groups and see which group can come up with most questions.

Unit Assessment Question

Intermediate 1: Outcome 3:
"The scientific method is the best way to work out what is true" Do you agree? Give two reasons for your answer.

Intermediate 2: Outcome 1:
Describe what you understand by "The Scientific Method".

Sample Exam Question

Intermediate 1:
How does the scientific method help to explain the world we live in? (4)

Intermediate 2:
"Scientific research should always be objective". What do you think this statement means? (6)

Homework

Find out about the life and work of Galileo Galilei. Why is he a good example of the use of the scientific method?

Funtime

Turn the scientific method into a song. Performing it would really help your class to remember it in the exam!

The Religious Method

Catholics, Protestants, Orthodox, Anglicans, Baptists, Methodists, Quakers, Adventists, Congregationalists, True Jesus Church, Brethren, Salvation Army, Evangelicals, Presbyterians, Wesleyan Reform, United Reformed, Reformed Presbyterians, Free, Wee Free, Church of England, Church of Scotland, Church of Ireland, Episcopalian . . . All Christians.
Now, as for the other faiths . . .

Task

Make a list of as many different Christian groups and denominations as you can. Now do the same for as many religions as you can. School year finished yet?

A Method?

It's quite easy for scientists to work out what's "true". The scientific method is agreed wherever science is done. But for religious people it's a bit different. There's no one way to work out what's true. This is obvious when you think about how many religions there are, and also how many varieties of belief there are even within one religion. This variety shows that they all have different ways of believing or following what they believe. But this gives us the problem of which one(s) to believe? As far as religion itself is concerned, here are some of the possibilities:

◆ All religions are true. They are just different ways of handling and expressing the truth

◆ None of the religions are true

◆ One of the religions is true and all the others are false

◆ Some of the religions are true and others are false.

As far as the Christian religion is concerned, it is split into many groupings. These denominations can be very different. Many of them claim to be the "best" version of Christianity. Some claim that they are a "better" way of being a Christian than others.

The Religious Method

Some just say that they are a different way of living as a Christian – no better, no worse than any other.

So how did all this difference come about? There's a lot of history involved, and it gets quite complicated sometimes. But it usually boils down to one thing – a different way (or method) of deciding what is true and what isn't. All Christians follow the same Bible (more or less), they all believe in God and his son Jesus, they all pray and so on ... and yet there are these differences. There is no one religious method, so how do religious people work out what is true?

The Woman

My king was lying on his couch, and my perfume filled the air with fragrance. My lover has the scent of myrrh as he lies upon my breasts ...

The Man

... your breasts are like gazelles, twin deer feeding among lilies ... the taste of honey is on your lips my darling; your tongue is milk and honey for me ... What a wonderful girl you are! How beautiful are your feet in sandals. The curve of your thighs is like the work of an artist. A bowl is there that never runs out of spiced wine. A sheaf of wheat is there, surrounded by lilies ... You are as graceful as a palm-tree, and your breasts are like clusters of dates. I will climb the palm tree and pick its fruit. To me your breasts are like bunches of grapes ...

Song of Songs: *Good News Bible*

Understanding the Bible

Imagine you had read this out in class without explaining what it was. It might have raised an eyebrow or two! It sounds very much like a slightly old-fashioned erotic love-poem – and it's in the Bible. What's going on?

◆ Is it just what it looks like? A sexy poem about the love between a man and a woman?

◆ Is it a symbolic explanation

94

of the relationship between God and his people, or Jesus and the Christian Church?

◆ Is it the Bible's way of saying "sex is great!"?

There are many disagreements between different Christians about this book in the Bible and what its point is. This shows up one of the problems about being Christian – how do you understand the Bible?

The Bible was written over many thousands of years. The Old Testament was only finalised as one book around 100 AD. What was in the New Testament wasn't completely agreed until the 4th century AD. Even when it was being put together there was disagreement about what should be "in" and what shouldn't. You'll find some versions of the Bible with extra books in it. These are the apocrypha and have wonderful names like the *Book of Tobit*, and the *Book of Bel and the Dragon*.

So what is, and isn't, holy scripture isn't as straightforward as you might think. Christians use the Bible in many different ways. But almost all Christians think that the Bible is one of the most important ways to find out what is true, what God wants, and how you should live your life as a Christian. But the Bible's a complicated book – understanding it isn't easy ...

Noah's Ark – fuzzy felt variety

In primary school you might have looked at the Noah's Ark story. But how? Did you read the story, make a frieze, sing some songs, make a fuzzy felt display? Did you ever discuss;

◆ What were the people doing that was so bad that God decided to kill them all?

◆ Why did God kill wee babies in the flood – what could they have done wrong?

◆ How did Noah get all the animals in one boat – and stop them from eating each other?

Maybe if you'd talked about these questions in Primary One or Two you'd have found yourself waking up with horrible nightmares! Obviously there are different "layers" of understanding in the Bible – any story can be read as just a story, or as something with far deeper meanings.

Task

Devise a way to teach primary children about the Noah's Ark story where you get them *really* thinking about what the story means.

SCIENCE AND BELIEF

A Method for Understanding the Bible

The Good News Bible suggests the following:

Stage One – Understand: What the passage you're reading actually says? Why was it written? What words were used? What do the words mean?

Stage Two – Explain: What did it mean to the people who first heard it? How does it compare with other Bible passages? If it's not clear, can anything else in the Bible help make it clearer?

Stage Three – Apply: Are there situations today where we could apply the same teaching? What should we do about what we've read?

This means that the Bible can be interpreted in many ways. This is even more likely to be the case when you think that there are totally different ways of understanding what the Bible is ...

> ## Task
>
> Choose a Bible passage completely at random. Now try to understand it using this set of stages.

The Inspired Word of God

Many Christians believe that every word in the Bible was written by people who were writing what God told them to write. This is God's actual word to humanity – so obviously it has to be taken seriously. Everything you need to help you in life is there in the Bible – God's direct teaching. The only problem is that this can still be understood in (at least!) two ways;

Literal understanding: Every word is true, it can't be wrong because it's God's word. If it said that God created the universe

God's direct teaching

in six days then he did – in exactly that amount of time. Many Christians think this approach is the best one, because you don't have to choose what to take seriously in the Bible and what to ignore.

Liberal understanding: This view says that the Bible needs to be understood in a more flexible way. Some stories are obviously true, but some are obviously poetry, or metaphor or allegory ... You can't interpret everything in the same way. Some liberals go further and say that the Bible is ...

A Book closely tied to the world of its writers

The Bible contains a great deal of different kinds of writing. It is too simplistic just to say that every word is absolutely true. We live in an ever-changing world. Things today are very different to the times of the Bible. Some things might still apply, but others don't. The people who put the Bible together made choices about what to keep in it and what not to keep in it. Their choices were human choices – some right, some wrong.

The world of the Bible didn't include genetic engineering and the ability to make nuclear weapons – so we shouldn't expect it to say anything directly about these. But it does give us general principles to follow – say about whether war is right or wrong – this can apply at any time. But it's up to us to work out the meaning for ourselves, not just blindly follow the Bible word for word.

Context

One key feature of understanding the Bible is taking things in context. This means not picking out sentences or phrases and separating them from the "bigger picture" that the whole chapter, verse or book is about. It's been said that you can find a Bible passage to support anything, but only if you take Bible teachings out of context.

Sometimes it's difficult to know what the context was when it was written, and you

The importance of context

SCIENCE AND BELIEF

have to be careful about how you understand things – but taking things out of context is sometimes one of the main reasons for Christians disagreeing about what the Bible teaching means.

But … many Christians can't spend hours trying to work out what the original passage means. Sometimes you might even have to be able to read the original Greek or Hebrew versions to really understand what's going on … if you can't, what do you do? You turn to the next part of the Christian "Method".

Authority

This means that others help you to work out what is true. In different churches it's done in different ways – but it all comes to the same thing: people study the Bible carefully, match it up with the way things have been done in that church and then come up with teachings for you to follow. You're still free to make your own decisions, but at least it gives you some guidance. This can be done in different ways;

In some churches, it might just be the Priest or Pastor of the church. He or she has studied long and hard to make sure they understand what Christianity is all about. Every week they might give a sermon about the faith. They might also run other teaching classes.

Sometimes it's more formal. In the Roman Catholic Church, the Pope takes advice about matters of faith from committees of priests, scholars and specialists in certain areas. He then gathers all their work together and issues guidance to Roman Catholics

The Pope and Bishops who share his responsibility for teaching

all over the world. These then become "the Church's view on . . . ". Roman Catholics are invited to follow the advice of these instructions.

Every year in the Church of Scotland, special committees are put together. Again, these are ministers, scholars and specialists in particular areas. These committees make reports about their discussions. This goes to the yearly meeting of the Church called the General Assembly (like a government of the Church). They vote on the reports and make changes if needed. This then becomes guidance for everyday Christians. It becomes "The Church's view on . . . "

There's also Tradition (with a capital T!). This means the things which a Church has always done – or always believed. Many Christians think some things shouldn't change just because the times are changing. Some truths about Christianity are timeless. These Traditions help Christians to work out what is true, and what is the Christian thing to do.

Authority could also mean listening to the beliefs and teachings of fellow Christians. Christianity shouldn't be a faith for loners – it's seen as a family. In any family, the other members should help you to grow up. Sometimes the teachings from these authorities might go against what you "feel" is right. What do you do then?

Prayer

Many Christians believe this is one of the most powerful parts of the "religious method". This is direct communication with God. If you want to know what is true, or what is the Christian thing to do, then . . . ask. But there are even different views in Christianity about this!

Many Christians believe that if you ask you shall get exactly what you ask for. Some believe that prayers are answered in a less obvious way. If you have faith that God will respond to your prayer, then it is probably a good way to work out what you should do in any particular situation – you pray, you get an answer, you do what you're told.

Prayer doesn't have to be long-winded and big-worded. It can be quite simple and straightforward – some Christians will say that you don't even need to say it out loud, you can just think it – God knows what you're thinking. Of course, what you ask for has to be sensible. It shouldn't be something that God might not want for you. For example, you probably shouldn't pray to win the lottery – unless maybe you were going to give it to charity!

The Religious Method

How (and if) prayers are answered is a matter of discussion in Christianity. There are many stories of prayers being answered in strange ways – or in miraculous ways ... but there are just as many stories of prayers not being answered at all. Some believe that it's just coincidence. Nick Blair, a school chaplain, says;

"Yes, you could say that it is 'just coincidence', but I can tell you that the more I pray, the more 'coincidences' seem to happen!"

Answered prayers

Nick and a group of volunteers were in Albania. They were there to help children. They were in a truck traveling over a high mountain pass. The snow was falling heavily, the visibility was next to nothing. The road ahead couldn't be seen. If they missed it, the truck would go over the edge – they'd probably have died. So they prayed for God's help. Just afterwards the driver said he could see tracks ahead. They were spaced as far apart as the truck's wheels. The truck ahead which must have made them couldn't have been far ahead or the tracks would've been covered with the fast-falling snow. The tracks meant they could follow the road safely and get down the other side of the mountain. But ... in Albania at the time there could only have been a couple of other trucks that big in the whole country. No one at any point on the road ahead could remember seeing another truck ... The "truck" that saved their lives. Coincidence?

Now if it was just a simple case of praying then hearing a big voice from the sky, then maybe things would be quite easy for the Christian. But it usually doesn't work that way. Sometimes the answer to a prayer isn't very clear. What too, if it seemed like a strange answer? What if you thought the answer to a prayer was that you should go out into the street and kill the first person you saw? Obviously you'd need to check such an "answer" out.

Living the Life

Remember, science is about testing out your hypotheses in real situations. So's the Christian faith. You put all the different ways of working out what's true and what is the right thing to do ... Bible Study, Authority, Tradition, Prayer ... And you put them into practice. Then you can work out how they can help you in your daily life. Do they help you to be a better Christian? Do they help you to understand the world in which you live? Do they help you to know what's true?

Christians talk about their religion as a "living faith". Sometimes you learn by doing – or even by your mistakes! This is just like the scientific method. You might also ask yourself "What would Jesus do?" – then you'd try to do the same yourself. You see what happens and then you modify your actions depending on the result. Religion can be "trial and error" too.

It's not easy!

Just like the scientific method, there can be problems with the religious method. It's not easy to work out what's true and what's right. There are lots of things to think about. You might need to get hold of a lot of different evidence and opinions. The religious method means putting all these different elements together and trying to make sense of them. Maybe it's not surprising that there are so many religions – and so many differences of opinion even inside a religion.

Task

Do you think that prayer works? Discuss this in groups or do a search on the internet – what arguments are there here for and against the "power of prayer"?

SCIENCE AND BELIEF

Source A

The rise of modern science posed a threat to theology, both in ... its content and ... its method. The content of modern science conflicted with a theology worked out in terms of medieval cosmology. The scientific method represented a rejection of a [systems of beliefs] based on authority. There were only two options at that time: to ignore the advance of [new scientific findings] or to insulate theology in one way or another from the threat of science ... If dialogue between science and theology is to be possible, especially if it is to be a two-way conversation, it is important to show that the disciplines are similar enough to be able to speak to one another and learn from one another.

N Murphy, in Religion & Science: History, Method, Dialogue Richardson & Wildman (Eds) Routledge; London 1996. pp 153 & 158

Comments

This suggests that when science was new and developing, the religious method was nothing but listening to authority. Ordinary people really only had the choice about whether to believe the traditional teachings of their faith, or the new findings of science. This might be why there was so much disagreement and confusion at the time — and perhaps why there's still sometimes a feeling of religion having to "defend" itself. But Murphy is saying that the religious method and the scientific method are not opposites. They share common features. So, each can learn something from the other.

Source B

Thomas deserved his [row] ... But I cannot think of a statement more foreign to ... Science ... than Jesus' celebrated [telling-off] of Thomas: "blessed are they that have not seen, and yet have believed". A skeptical attitude towards ... Authority, combined with a demand for direct evidence ... represents the first commandment of proper scientific procedure. Poor Doubting Thomas. At his crucial ... Moment he acted in a most admirable way for one style on inquiry – but in the wrong magisterium. He [demonstrated] the key principle of science while operating within the different magisterium of faith

SJ Gould Rocks of Ages (Jonathon Cape, London 2001 p 16)

Comments

Gould's book argues that science and religion should get on fine provided they stick to their own methods. He uses the Bible story of "Doubting Thomas" (see John: 20, 24–29). Thomas acted like a scientist, by asking Jesus to provide evidence for who he was – and that he had come back from the dead. But Jesus seemed to say that the only evidence needed was your faith – scientific proof wasn't relevant here (and yet he provided that for Thomas). Jesus seems to be teaching that in some things – matters of belief, the religious method means that you only need to believe – you don't need proof in the scientific sense.

Facts and Figures

◆ There are estimated to be over a billion Christians on planet earth

◆ The Christian Bible is the world's best-selling book

◆ Until recently, the Pope was believed to be *infallible* in all things – that means whatever he said was *always* right (but only when he is speaking on matters of faith)

Activities

Knowledge and Understanding

Intermediate 1

1 This is the religious method. Match the phrases with the right descriptions:
Bible reading: Finding out what's true directly from God
Authority: Trying to put Christianity into practice and then seeing what happens
Prayer: Finding out from the Holy Scriptures what is true
Living the Life: Following the teachings of great or important Christians – or of a church

2 In question 1, can any of the descriptions match more than one phrase? Which one(s) Why?

3 Give one explanation why the book "Song of Songs" might be in the Bible.

4 Copy and complete:

The story of Noah's __ shows that Bible _____ can be_____ at many different "levels". What you understand as the meaning of the story depends on how you _____ it.

      stories   Ark   interpret understood

5 What would a Christian mean if he said "The Bible is the inspired word of God"?

6 Some people think the Bible is "closely tied to the world of its writers". What does this mean?

7 Name two possible types of Authority which a Christian might follow.

8 What happened to Nick Blair? What do you think about this?

9 Copy and complete using the right choices where the * is.
(NB You might not need to choose one of the choices – the right answer could be all of them – and you pick the one you agree with!)

Christians believe that prayer is a good part of the *religious/scientific method. They believe that it is a way of *talking to/ignoring God. Sometimes prayers are answered *directly/lightly. Other times it isn't so obvious. When Christians receive answers to prayer they should *always/never/sometimes follow it. Some people think answered prayers are just *coincidence/God's work.

10 State one way in which the religious method can be like the Scientific Method.

11 Read Source A and the Comments on it again. Does Murphy say that the religious and scientific methods are opposites?

12 Read Source B again. Why did Thomas get a row from Jesus?

Activities continued

Intermediate 2

1 How would you explain the fact that there are many religions in the world?

2 Why do you think Christians don't all agree about everything?

3 Explain why some people might think the Bible is a complicated way to find out what's true.

4 Give one reason why Christians might interpret the Bible differently.

5 What's the difference between a literal and a liberal understanding of the Bible?

6 In what way would it matter if the Bible was inspired or not?

7 Why is context important when studying the Bible? Explain your answer fully.

8 How might a Roman Catholic and a member of the Church of Scotland work out what their Church's view on anything was?

9 State one advantage and one disadvantage of using prayer as a way of working out what's true.

10 What are the similarities and differences between the religious method and the scientific method?

11 In Source A, what explanation is there for the disagreements between science and religion when modern science was just beginning?

12 In Source B, what evidence is there that Thomas was acting according to the scientific method?

Practical Activities

1 Find the books of the apocrypha. Choose one and read it. Write a brief report about its contents. Explain also why it is in some versions of the Bible and not others.

2 As a group, make up a short lesson on the Noah's Ark story which you could use with Primary 3 pupils. How could you make sure that they started to think not only about the content of the story, but about what the meanings behind it might be?

3 Choose a selection of Bible passages in consultation with your teacher. Now, using the "Method for Understanding the Bible" on page 96, work through the method in relation to the passage you're looking at. Write down what you find and share this with other members of your class.

4 The virgin birth is often a source of discussion (and disagreement) in Christianity. Mary was called a parthenos (Παρθενος). Why does the exact meaning of the word matter so much? Do some research, then discuss your findings in class.

5 Have a class debate based on Nick Blair's story on page 100. "This house believes that Nick Blair's story proves there's a God".

6 Write a list of things you think a Christian should be able to pray for and things he/she shouldn't be able to pray for. (For example, should a Christian be able to pray to win the lottery – or to save his life if he's in a train that's about to crash?) For each of your choices explain why you think this is something which you should/should not be able to pray for.

Unit Assessment Question

Intermediate 1: Outcome 1:
What is "The Religious Method"?

Intermediate 2 Outcome 3:
How far do you agree that the religious method is better than the scientific method for deciding what is real?

Sample Exam Question

Intermediate 1:
In what ways might religious belief help us to understand the world? (4)

Intermediate 2:
"The Religious Method is a better way to find out the truth than the Scientific Method" Do you agree? (6)

Homework

Read the story of Doubting Thomas (John: 20, 24–29). In 50 words, explain what you think this teaches about the relationship between the Religious and Scientific methods.

Funtime

The Noah's Ark story is often done as a frieze in schools. Make your own frieze . . . with a difference about the story. It should be more like a Salvador Dali painting than a children's frieze. (Ask your RMPS teacher!)

The Beginning of the Universe: Science

So What?

How did the universe begin? Maybe it's not the first thing you think about when you wake up, but for many people it is an important question – it goes right to the heart of what it means to be a human.

◆ How everything began is probably the biggest mystery of all. It's part of human nature to find the answers to things

◆ Knowing how the universe began might help us in ways we didn't expect. For example, maybe this knowledge will improve human life in some way?

◆ Some people think that if the universe is just an accident then there's not much point to life. Some think that if the universe was made, then there is. Most people want to know why we are here – maybe finding out how the universe began can help us answer the question: "What is life for?"

The mystery of the universe

◆ People have always wondered whether there is something controlling the universe. Some call this God. If God created the universe then that could be quite an important thing to know about. If there's a point to the universe then maybe how we live our daily lives matters more.

If we say that the question of how the universe began doesn't really matter, then we'd have to ask ourselves, what does? If we don't think how everything began is important, maybe we shouldn't bother getting out of bed in the morning, just lie around all day for 70 years or so waiting to die.

Task

Discuss: Who cares how the Universe began?

The Big Bang

The science of how the universe might have started is fairly complicated ... so let's keep it as simple as possible. About 15,000 million years ago, there was a massive explosion. At this point – and no one really knows why – everything began. The explosion caused everything to start, all matter in the universe began. But it was not only matter that was created at the Big Bang, but space and time too. This means:

◆ There was no *before* the Big Bang because there was no time for the *before* to be in (!)

◆ There was *nowhere* for the Big Bang to happen because there was *nowhere* for it to be (!)

After this explosion, all the matter created expanded very quickly. Forces like gravity eventually pulled matter together in clumps. These clumps of gas, space "dust" and the elements became stars, galaxies, and planets like our own. They even became us ... we are all made of stardust.

Now, did the Big Bang *have* to happen? No one really knows.

Obviously no one saw it, so all our evidence has to be worked out from what we can "see" today. Scientists call this inference or deductive reasoning.

Suppose you walk into a room and there's a pie on the table. The pie is quite warm, but not piping hot. It must be the case that someone has been in the room and left the pie. They've obviously been there during the last hour, otherwise the pie would be cold (assuming the sun's not shining on the pie!). You haven't seen the person, you have no direct evidence of them, but you can work out from the heat of the pie that they have been there, and roughly how long ago they left. Maybe if there's a bite out of the pie you could also work out how big their mouth is.

The evidence for the Big Bang goes along the same lines. You can work out from what's around in the universe today, what things would probably have been like at the moment of the Big Bang. You could also work out that the Big Bang probably happened. How?

Solving a mystery

Matter in the universe is moving apart at a known rate: If we work out how fast things are moving apart and then work back in time, we get to a point where everything must have exploded in the first place (the Big Bang). Imagine sitting in class and having a piece of chalk hit you on the back of the head. You could work out the direction it came from, as well as how hard it was thrown (according to how much it hurt!). You could do all of this without having to see it being thrown in the first place. Scientists can do the same thing with the Big Bang.

The amount of material in the universe is just what you'd expect after a Big Bang: A good chef can taste something and then describe what's in it. An excellent chef could maybe even tell you how much of everything was there. The universe is like that. The helium, hydrogen, and all the other elements exist in just the right proportion that you'd get if there had been a Big Bang in the first place.

Background radiation present today is what you'd expect if there was a Big Bang: This is a bit like the pie above. Imagine a bonfire which is now just faintly glowing. You could work out how hot the bonfire had been, how long it burned and so on, by working back from the information you now have. The universe still contains this "leftover heat" from the original Big Bang. This "proves" that the Big Bang happened.

> **Task**
>
> In your own words, summarise the evidence for the Big Bang.

So what ... again

If the Big Bang is true, then there are some consequences ...

The Big Bang might mean that the universe just happened. It didn't need to happen and there's no particular point in its existence. Nothing caused it, except the "blind" laws of nature. Some people think that if there's no point to the universe then how we live doesn't really matter. Others don't agree. They say that we can still live good lives, even if there's no real "point" to the universe.

the origin of the universe proved surprising

The origin of the universe proved surprising

The Big Bang was so vast and so incredibly powerful that it makes everything we do in our daily lives seem a bit tiny. We're just one wee planet in an ocean of space ... so we don't really matter very much. Maybe we don't have that much control over anything – the laws of nature are far more powerful than we could ever be. Others might say that size doesn't matter! Maybe the fact that we can understand something about how our universe began is special – maybe we're the only living things in the universe who can – nothing to be ashamed of there! We're still free to behave however we like, no matter what the laws of nature are.

But of course, if it's all chance and accident, then that might mean there's no God behind it all. This might worry some people. But not all.

Just a Theory?

It's important to remember that science is always moving on. Good scientists know that our ideas about how things work can change when new evidence arises. Maybe in 100 years no one will believe the Big Bang theory, because a better explanation might have replaced it. But for the moment, the Big Bang is the best explanation we have.

Source A

We, who are children of the universe – animated stardust – can . . . reflect on the nature of the same universe, even to the extent of glimpsing the rules on which it runs. How we have become linked into this cosmic dimension is a mystery. Yet the linkage cannot be denied. What does it mean? . . . I cannot believe that our existence in this universe is a mere quirk of fate, an accident of history . . . Our involvement is too intimate. The existence of [humans] may count for nothing, but the existence of mind in some organism on some planet in the universe is surely a fact of fundamental significance. Through conscious beings, the universe has generated self-awareness. This can be no trivial detail, no minor by-product of mindless, purposeless forces. We are truly meant to be here.

Paul Davies *The Mind of God* (Penguin Books 1992, p 232)

Comments

Davies shows that he believes there is some point to the universe. Because humans are aware of themselves and because they can consciously think about how everything began, maybe humans have a special part to play. Maybe this ability of humans is the universe's way of becoming aware of itself! This gives humans a very important part in the universe. Davies does not deny the possibility of the Big Bang, but he does think that there's more to it all than just pure chance. There's a purpose in it all . . . somewhere.

Source B

Even if there is only one possible unified theory, it is just a set of rules and equations. What is it that breathes fire into the equations and makes a universe for them to describe? The usual approach of science of constructing a mathematical model cannot answer the questions of why there should be a model to describe. Why does the universe go to all the bother of existing? Up to now, most scientists have been too occupied with the development of new theories that describe what the universe is to question why. However, if we do discover a complete theory, it should in time be understandable in broad principle by everyone, not just a few scientists . . . then we shall all be able to take part in the discussion . . . of why it is that we and the universe exist. If we find the answer to that, then it would be the ultimate triumph of human reason – for then we would know the mind of God.

Stephen Hawking *A Brief History of Time* (Bantam Books 1988)

Comments

Hawking is searching for a unified theory – something which will explain the origins of everything. He doesn't seem to think that mathematical explanations on their own go far enough yet. He thinks an explanation for how the Universe began might well be found, and he thinks that when it is, it could be really much more simple than we expect. Hawking still isn't sure whether the answer will allow people to carry on believing in a God or not, but he does think that human intelligence can take us very close to answering the big questions.

◆ Edwin Hubble (1889–1953) was the first scientist to show that galaxies are moving away from each other

◆ There are more stars in the sky than grains of sand on earth

◆ The temperature at the moment of the Big Bang was probably around 10,000 million degrees

Facts and Figures

SCIENCE AND BELIEF

Activities

Knowledge and Understanding

Intermediate 1

1 Mr X thinks that how the universe began is an important question. Give two (sensible!) reasons why he might think this.

2 Copy and Complete:
About _____ million years ago, there was a massive _____. At this point – and no one really knows why – _____ began. The explosion caused everything to start, all matter in the _____ today was begun then. But it's even more odd than that, because it was not only matter that was created at the Big Bang, but _____ and time too.

> explosion   15,000   universe
> space   everything

3 Match up the word with the right explanation:

Big Bang – the information you have which you use to "prove something".
Expanded – the force which pulled matter together in clumps.
Gravity – The theory scientists use to explain how the universe began.
Evidence – the word which explains how the universe moved apart (and still is).

4 If you found a hot pie in an empty room, what information could you work out using the pie as evidence?

5 Put this set of statements into the right order.

  i   So it must have started at one point
  ii This point is called the Big Bang
  iii Scientists know that everything in the universe is moving apart
  iv We can work back to this point
  v This is happening at a known rate

6 Complete these two sentences using either information in the text or your own views;

  a If the universe is an accident then . . .
  b If the universe was created on purpose then . . .

7 In Source A, Paul Davies says that "We are truly meant to be here". What does he mean? Do you agree?

8 Read Source B again, and the commentary on it. From what you have read, do you think Stephen Hawking believes in God?

Intermediate 2

1 How might knowing how the universe began make any difference to human life?

2 When do scientists think the Big Bang happened?

Activities continued

3 Why is the question what happened before the Big Bang a difficult one?

4 What pulled the matter together in clumps after the Big Bang?

5 What do scientists mean by inference or deductive reasoning?

6 Describe, in your own words, the three pieces of evidence scientists have to show that the Big Bang probably happened.

7 Why might some people call the Big Bang an "accident"?

8 Some people think the size of the universe makes humans seem insignificant. What do they mean?

9 Why might the Big Bang theory not be around in 100 years or so?

10 What does Paul Davies say might be really special about humans?

11 When does Stephen Hawking think we might "know the mind of God"?

Practical Activities

1 Write out a dialogue between two people (anyone you like!). Which starts like this . . .

   MEL: I think the universe began with a Big Bang.
   TONY: You know, I really don't care how it began.
   MEL: How can you say that . . .

2 Design your own poster or information leaflet explaining the Big Bang theory as simply as you can.

3 Find out about the life and ideas of Edwin Hubble; Fred Hoyle; Albert Einstein; Stephen Hawking. Write up a mini project showing how they helped the Big Bang theory along.

4 Do a search on the web using the phrase "Big Bang theory". Write a short report of your findings.

5 Have a class discussion/debate: "What is life for?"

6 Make a list for yourself of "Questions in life which matter to me". Think of as many as you can. Compare these with others in your class.

Unit Assessment Question

Intermediate 1: Outcome 1:
Why might the Big Bang theory be a problem for people who believe in God?

Intermediate 2: Outcome 3:
"You cannot question the truth of the Big Bang theory". To what extent do you agree?

Sample Exam Question

Intermediate 1:
How does science explain the origins of the universe? (4)

Intermediate 2:
"The Big Bang theory is the best explanation we have for the question of how the Universe began". How far do you agree? (6)

Homework

Do your own research. Ask as many people as you can how they think the universe began. Try to get them to explain their beliefs as fully as they can. How many people say the Big Bang but have trouble explaining what this is? Be prepared to report your findings to the the class.

Funtime

Try to get some humour into this task as far as possible! Write and perform a sketch as follows:

Cyril Scientist thinks everyone should be as interested in how the universe began as he is – and he really is (Einstein's theories of special relativity are light bedtime reading for him). So, he goes round people's houses, knocking on their doors to explain the Big Bang, and why it matters to us all. As you can imagine, he gets some funny reactions. On this particular day he knocks on Big Bill's door. Big Bill doesn't really care about the Big Bang (or about much else really), but he decides to have a laugh by getting into conversation (of sorts) with Cyril . . .

The Beginning of the Universe: Christian Belief

Right aff there wiznae anythin'. The universe wiz empty. The earth wiz jist a big ba' ... right bare so it wiz. An' the watter, it wiz a' ower the place. Black as tar it wiz anall. The Big Man in the Sky – that's God so tae yoo an' me – says: "c'moan, a wee bit light therr if ye don't mind". An' right enuff, it got pure dead shinin' ... gleamin' and sparklin' as well. God wiz well chuffed. Then He says; " You oan that side, your night so ye are. You, aye, you therr, your day". Day Wan. Next, He pit oan a roof so tae speak. It fair kept yon watters away fae each other. Day Two. He shoogled the solid bits intae wan place. Noo it's the earth. He wiz getting fair carried away wi' himsel' noo right enuff. He wiz the cat's pyjamas and nae mistake. Then He made the wee plants and floo'ers. Day Three. Then he did the Sun and the Moon – so we ken when wan days' done an' anurrer yin's kicked aff. Day Four. Next, He cooked up the slippy things in the watter, an' the wee burdies as well. Day Five. Next aff' millions o' animals. Wee fluffy wans, big hairy wans, scary wans, even pure dead ugly wans. An' then, did He no go an' make us tae tap it a' aff. Says, "right, yous are in charge, an' ye better dae it right" ... jeez. Day Six.
Oan Day Seven He pit his feet up, and telt us tae dae the same.

Based on Genesis: 2, 4

The creation story

The truth is in there

This is a (slightly unusual) version of the creation story in the Bible. Many people believe that the universe began in exactly the way it is written in the book of Genesis in the Bible. Such people are Creationists. They believe the Bible is literally true. So, if it says that God created the universe in six days, then that's what it means – God took 144 hours (or 8,640 minutes) to create everything that exists today. Also, he made it the way it is and it hasn't changed since. You can even work out from the Bible exactly how old the world is. Many people today (even other Christians) think this way of understanding the Bible is wrong. But what do the Creationists think?

◆ If you start fiddling about with the Bible, then you're deciding for yourself what's true and what isn't. Why would it be written if it wasn't true? If you believe some of it, but not all, how will you decide which bits to believe and which bits to ignore?

◆ Christianity is a faith. This means believing without having to have what you believe in proved to you. People who don't believe the Genesis story happened the way the Bible says it did aren't showing much faith.

◆ God can do anything. Just because humans couldn't create a universe in six days doesn't mean that God can't.

◆ What makes theories like the Big Bang easier to believe than the creation story? Is it any more strange to think that God made everything than to think that it just happened with a great big explosion?

Are the Creationists coping?

So how do Creationists deal with the evidence for the Big Bang?

◆ It could all be a test of faith. God has put it there on purpose to see if we keep on believing.

◆ Maybe it's the work of the Devil – put there to test us again.

◆ There are still lots of gaps in our knowledge. Even if there was a Big Bang we still don't know why.

◆ No one was there to see it. The "evidence" of science is just one way of looking at things. The Bible has been shown to be true in so many ways – why should it be wrong about the creation?

◆ How does a belief in the Big Bang help us live our lives? It doesn't make any difference to whether we're good or bad. Believing that God made everything at least means there's some point and meaning to it all.

One way of looking at Creationists is that they just don't get it – they're running away from the evidence. On the other hand, maybe they're right. Maybe the way they stick to their beliefs in the face of hard science isn't so strange. Maybe that's what faith is about. In the USA, some schools teach Creation Science, where the Genesis story is the scientific explanation of how the universe began. Here, Big Bang science is thought of as just plain wrong.

Creationist belief in the Bible story is an act of faith. But they might find they have to defend this belief every time new scientific evidence is discovered if they try to make creationism "scientific". Their belief in God won't be affected by the Big Bang, because – in the words of Victor Meldrew – they don't belieeeeeve it.

Task

What do you think of the Creationists' argument? List the points for and against it in your opinion.

Bending it a bit

Some Christians think you need to be a bit more flexible. They believe that the Bible is true, but that doesn't mean every word as it is written. These Christians also have faith, but they have faith that the Bible story matches up with science – maybe even in some way that we don't yet understand. They could say;

◆ Look at the creation story. It follows the same pattern as the scientific explanation for the beginning of the universe. How could the writers of the Bible have known that when they wrote it?

◆ The Bible isn't meant to explain the exact details of how the universe began, just give a rough outline of the general picture.

◆ The Big Bang doesn't do away with the need for God. Something must have caused the Big Bang. Maybe God is the scientific explanation for the Big Bang!

◆ Maybe the Genesis story and the Big Bang are both true. Maybe humans aren't clever enough to put the two together and make any sense of it.

Many Christians think being flexible like this is the best way. It means that you can still believe in God creating everything but also accept the evidence for the Big Bang. Some think this is a bit dodgy. It has to be Big Bang or God's creation, you can't have it both ways. You can't just bend Bible stories to fit with the latest science. If you do, what's next? Some Christians don't like this approach because it leads to a "god of the gaps" way of thinking. As science explains more and more, there's less and less room for God. So these Christians will have to squeeze God into smaller and smaller spaces.

Task

Do you think these flexible Christians are being true to their beliefs? Discuss.

Means What?

These Christians can believe in the Bible and in science, they just have to fit one into the other. This means they don't have to keep defending their beliefs, because science isn't a threat to them. The Bible is true, so is the Big Bang theory. How they can both be true isn't something humans can understand – only God can. Science shows how God works – and some of the things it doesn't explain can be put down to God.

Two different worlds

Some Christians think that the evidence for the Big Bang is so powerful that it must be true. But that doesn't make the Bible wrong, just different. They think that the Bible shouldn't be read as if it was a science book. It's not meant to tell you *how* the universe began. It is meant to tell you *why* it began and what that *means* for us all. They might say that the Genesis story is poetry, or metaphor. It is a simple way to pass on the message:

> *God made the universe and he gave humans*
> *a special place in it.*

Two different worlds

The Beginning of the Universe: Christian Belief

These Christians would say that you can't compare the Bible and the Big Bang theory, because they're two different things.

I Love You

You're sitting with your girlfriend on a moonlit night. The stars above are twinkling sweetly. You turn to her, holding her hand in yours, shielding her with your arm from the crisp night air. Your eyes meet. You start to speak ... "Morag ... " your palms are sweating ... "Morag ... I ... I just wanted to say". She looks at you, an air of expectation, her breath held ... "Morag ... I love you ... I love you with all my brain".

Something not quite right here isn't there? Of course, you do love her with your brain. Your heart's just a pump which moves the blood round your body. Your brain does the thinking ... and the loving. But it doesn't sound right somehow does it?

Christians who think the Bible and the Big Bang theory are different ways of looking at the beginning of the universe are thinking in a similar way. The Big Bang is the logical, scientific way to explain how the universe began, but the Genesis story appeals to the human "heart". It is poetry which everyone can understand. It helps us know our place in life and gives us some idea of the power and love of God. It's a lot better than this;

In the beginning, when God created the universe, the earth was formless and void ... so God commanded:

$$\frac{\text{"N} + X2\theta\square\Sigma\square + \square\#\square\bigstar = 23/ >\square\square\approx - N/p2}{234 \cong \eta\Psi \neq / 4\text{"}}$$

Makes the Bible story really come to life, doesn't it?

> ### Task
> How would you reply to this statement if you were Morag?

Non-overlapping magisteria

This is what the Scientist Stephen Jay Gould calls it. Magisteria means your own "empire" – your turf so to speak. He says that religion and science should stick to their own home ground. Science can tell us how the universe began (the technical stuff) and religion can tell us what this *means* for us as humans and can suggest *why* the universe exists, and *who* started it. As long as scientists don't stray into religion, and religious people don't try to pretend that the Bible is science everything will be OK.

Means what?

These Christians read the Bible differently to the Creationists. They see lots of different kinds of writing in the Bible. Some of it says exactly what it means, other parts need a little more interpretation. Most of these Christians are perfectly happy for science to discover more about the Big Bang. This is because the more we know, the more amazing the whole thing is. This makes God all the more incredible, because he made it.

Source A — www.creationtips.ws

God **could** have used evolution to form life on earth (theistic evolution) if He had wanted to. But He didn't. If the Bible truly is the revealed Word of God, as Christians believe, then what God tells us in the Bible must be true. He tells us He created everything in six days — not evolved them over billions of years. He tells us He created all the different kinds of animals and plants "after their kind." This means He created mature animals and plants ready to reproduce more of their own kind. He tells us He created the first man from the dust of the ground — not from an ape-like creature. When reporters from newspapers or television stations want to find out what happened, they try to find an eyewitness who can tell them. In the same way, if we want to find out what happened at the beginning of the world, we should find out what the eyewitness says. Eyewitness says creation! God the Creator was the only eyewitness, and He tells us in the Bible's book of Genesis that He created things — they did not evolve.

Comments

This is from a Creationist website, though it calls itself Creationology. It argues throughout the site that science is wrong and the Bible is right. There are many references to science throughout the site, and challenges to the scientific explanations of the origins of the universe. Many of these challenges are based on the idea that the Bible is right in the first place. The creationist argument usually depends upon you accepting that the Bible is completely true, and if you do, all the rest of the creationist argument makes sense. But if you don't believe that the Bible is literally true (or don't believe in it at all), then you'll find some of the arguments difficult to take.

The Beginning of the Universe: Christian Belief

Source B

Creation? Although there are a large number of scientific arguments to be settled, today, the evidence for the Big Bang is considered overwhelming ... Science has pointed very clearly in the direction of the Big Bang creation of the Universe, but the cause of the Big Bang still remains very much an enigma ... Christians can equally contemplate the Big Bang and its aftermath and see there the planned work of God ... It will never be possible, or even necessary, to prove scientifically ... that [the universe] must be the work of God. But certainly the Big Bang theory fits well with the idea. As the creator, God .... Brings into existence what he has planned. And when God is finished with this process, what he has made speaks of God the Creator.

Jim Brooks *Origins of Life* (Lion Publishing 1985; pp 40–44)

Comments

Brooks presents all the scientific arguments for the Big bang, but sees no reason why they should push a creator God out of the way. In fact, he's really suggesting that the more we find out about the Big Bang, the more we understand the power of God. He doesn't think that there can ever be a scientific way to link God with the Big Bang. He doesn't think we need to do that anyway. The size, complexity and power of the Universe can only point to God the creator.

◆ In some schools in the USA, Creation Science is taught alongside, or instead of, traditional science

◆ Christians believe that God created the world out of nothing. Quantum physics seems to show that this might be possible

◆ By working through Adam's "family tree" in the Bible, the creation must have happened about 10,000 years ago

Facts and Figures

Activities

Knowledge and Understanding

Intermediate 1

1 Where, in the Bible, would you find the creation story?

2 Here are the events of the creation story. They are out of order though. Put them in the right order. 1 = first, 7 = last.

1 God makes animals and humans
2 God has a rest
3 God makes light and night and day
4 God makes the Sun and the Moon
5 God makes birds and sea creatures
6 God makes plants and flowers
7 God separates earth and sky

3 Copy and complete:

Some people believe the creation story in the _____ is literally true. They think that's exactly how it happened. These people are called _____. They don't need proof, it is just their _____.
Other Christians think that the Bible story is just a way of _____ something which is too complicated for us to understand. They think the Big ____ and the _____ story are both true.

**Creationists   Bible   explaining
Bang faith   Genesis**

4 Look at the bullet points on page 115. Choose one of the arguments which Creationists use to support their beliefs. Write this out in your own words.

5 Explain this sentence in your own words.

Many Christians believe that Science tells us *how* the universe began, but the Bible tells us *why*.

6 In Source A, the idea of an eyewitness is used to prove that the Bible story is true. How is this done? What do you think of this argument?

7 In Source B, why doesn't the writer think we need to prove a link between God and the Big Bang? What do you think?

Intermediate 2

1 In your own words, describe the Creation story as you find it in the Bible.

2 What does a Creationist think of this story? Why do they think this?

3 How might a Creationist argue that the Genesis story is just as believable as the Big Bang theory?

4 Creationists deal with the evidence for the Big Bang in certain ways. Describe two of these ways and state your own views about it.

5 What effect does the Big Bang theory have on the Creationist's belief in God?

6 Other Christians don't believe the Genesis story is literally true. What do they think?

7 These Christians might say that God is the scientific explanation for the Big Bang. What do you think they mean? What are your views on this?

8 What is meant by non-overlapping magisteria? How does it help some Christians deal with the Big Bang v Creation issue?

9 Read source A again. Explain what you think of the argument used here.

10 Read source B again. How does Brooks link God with the Big Bang?

Practical Activities

1 The Biblical creation story has been the subject of many works of art. Choose a part of the story and make your own representation of it artistically. You could do this as a drawing/painting. You could also use various items to create your own "sculpture" which represents a scene from the story. Use your imagination!

2 a Make a short leaflet which outlines the Creationist arguments for the beginning of the Universe. You could look up the Internet under the heading "creationism" for help.

   b Now do the same for Christians who accept the Big Bang theory, but seem to be able to believe this and in the Bible. You could use the following website to help you: www.cis.org.uk.

3 The version of the Genesis story on page 114 was written in a Scottish style (the author is from Clydebank after all). Read the original Genesis story and write it in a style which reflects where you live. For example;

   "Ken noo, it first there wis naehin'. A' hings wis . . . ".

   You could maybe use words from your own dialect. Alternatively you could re-write the story as a rhyming poem, or a rap . . .

   "Totally empty, so it was
   everywhere wet like chippy sauce
   the earth was formless there in space
   So God said 'light' and it was ace" . . .

4 Following your own further research into the Big Bang v Creationism, have a balloon debate. (throw each person out leaving the last one in who has the best argument.) There should be three people in the balloon:

- A Creationist Christian
- A Christian who thinks he can match up the Big Bang story with the Creation story
- A Christian who thinks science and Christianity should stick to what they know best

5 Create in your classroom a graffiti board. In the centre, should be the question "How did the Universe begin?". People should write their own views on the question around this. Perhaps you should ask others in school to come to your class and write their views . . . the local Minister/Priest . . . Some of your teachers . . . ?

6 Some people (Christians included) argue that the Bible can't be taken as always literally true because, if we did, it creates too many problems. Using the following examples, and perhaps using the Internet and other sources, discuss the following questions.

- How could all the animals fit into Noah's Ark?
- What did the animals on the Ark eat when they were at sea?
- Who did Adam and Eve's children marry?
- Why did God make so many beetles?
- Why are there fossils of long-dead species?
- Were there really dinosaurs?

Unit Assessment Question

Intermediate 1: Outcome 2:
Describe two ways a Christian might reply to the statement "The Big Bang theory proves that the Creation story is wrong".

Intermediate 2: Outcome 3:
How far do you agree that Christian beliefs about the origin of the universe are compatible with scientific accounts?

Sample Exam Question

Intermediate 1:
Why do some Christians not accept the scientific account of the origin of the universe? (4)

Intermediate 2:
"The Bible story of the creation could be right". To what extent do you agree? (6)

Homework

In 50 words, explain what you think of the Creationist view of the beginning of the universe.

Funtime

Ever seen a flick cartoon book? Use the order of events in the Genesis story to make your own. It's probably best to choose just one of the days, or it could take you a long time! Make sure that you don't offend the beliefs of anyone in your class, by drawing something they might think is unacceptable.

The Origin of Life: Science

John Burbleblott

The birth of John Burbleblott was unremarkable. So were his parents. So were his early years. It was only when he started school that things began to hot up. He seemed to know what the teacher was thinking before she did. Soon he would finish sentences off for people, or even answer their questions before they had asked them. "How does he do that?" Some thought. "Weird", others muttered. By the time he got to secondary school there wasn't much point in teaching him. By now, he was able to look at the title of a book and know every word it contained. In fact, when John walked into a library, all the words in the books in the library just transferred themselves into his head. One day he logged on to the Internet. Lo and behold, every website became part of John's memory – including the ones that weren't written yet.

But John wasn't daft. He knew that this strange power would be of interest to many people – governments, the military and so on. So, he used his powers to win the lottery – in every country where there was one. John Burbleblott became the richest man on planet earth. Obviously this was quite attractive to many people – including the opposite sex.

Before long, the now twenty-something John was a dad – many times over. Some of his children were born with his remarkable abilities and, over the years, pretty much followed in John's footsteps. Now, all over the world, there are Burbleblotts with these incredible powers. But they do tend to keep things quiet (they change their names regularly to avoid detection). There may be Burbleblotts around you right now. The way things are going though, in a thousand years or so there will be nothing but Burbleblotts. Ordinary punters like you and me will have died out and been replaced with these remarkable creatures . . .

Evolution by Natural Selection

Natural Selection is the scientific theory of how life on earth began and developed. It's a little like the Burbleblotts – the world eventually becomes populated mostly with Burbleblotts because they are best suited to the world in which they find themselves. The theory of Evolution by Natural Selection was developed by Charles Darwin (1809–1882). It goes like this:

John Burbleblott

◆ When two of a species mate, their offspring is a unique mixture of the DNA each of the two partners has

◆ DNA is the chemical information, or plan for you – it decides what colour of hair you'll have, what body shape you get and so on

◆ Every now and again, DNA mutates. This means that it changes slightly. This can happen for loads of reasons. It happens completely at random ... by chance. When it does happen, the offspring of any living thing becomes just a little different from its "parents"

◆ Sometimes this is a bad thing. The change might mean that the living thing can't survive like its parents did ... so it dies, and with it so does its dodgy and rather useless DNA

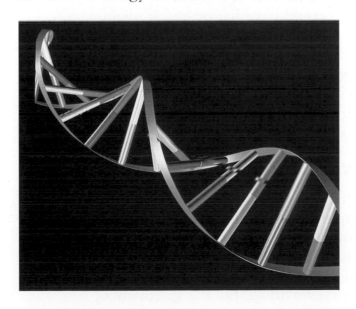

DNA

125

◆ Sometimes though, it's really useful. The mutant DNA gives the life-form something its parents didn't have. Something which makes it more likely to survive. So, it prospers. It produces its own offspring. Some of these have the mutant (really useful DNA)

◆ They too have offspring and pass on this useful DNA

◆ Before you know it there are loads of creatures around with this really useful DNA. They have a much better chance of survival than the creatures without it … so it ends up that there are more with this new DNA than with the old stuff. The ones with the old DNA fade away and the ones with the new really useful DNA become the stars in the show of life

◆ BUT … this only works provided the environment they live in is stable. If there are sudden changes, the benefits (advantages) of their really useful DNA might no longer apply

◆ With any luck, another "mutant" DNA type will arrive just in the nick of time. This one will have a better chance of survival in the new circumstances and so will replace the old really useful DNA with new even more useful DNA.

> **Task**
>
> In your own words, explain what is meant by Evolution by Natural Selection.

Beginnings?

If evolution is true, then it means that this is how life on earth developed, but how did it begin? According to the evolutionary theory it must have been the case that simpler organisms mutated into more complex ones. This means that inorganic materials must somehow have mutated into organic ones. Scientists aren't sure how this could have happened. It might have been that electrical storms somehow fused elements together into organic compounds and started off simple chains of amino acids (the building blocks of DNA). Over millions of years, these single celled organisms evolved by random mutation into the staggering variety of life there is today.

Darwin's Discovery

Darwin had a few career changes. His dad wanted him to be a priest, so he started studying religious studies, but gave up. To cut a long story short he ended up on a scientific research ship sailing the world studying nature. In Darwin's day, the Christian Church was really powerful. Science had to watch its step. The Church taught that God made everything, but the discovery of fossils of long-dead species made some people ask questions. For example, why did God make things and then kill them off?

Also, new things were being found out all the time about human and animal life. Humans seemed to share lots of the features of other living things. Had God run out of ideas during the creation? And, if he made everything as it is today, why did there seem to be some evidence of change and development in living things throughout the ages? Geology seemed to show that the earth was millions of years old, but the Bible seemed to say it was only thousands. What was going on?

Charles Darwin

Darwin's Big Clue

Darwin's travels finally got him to the Galapagos Islands in the South Pacific in 1835. Here he noticed something very odd. On three tiny islands there were finches. But on each island there was a different kind of finch. On one, the finch had a wee pointy beak. On another, a big chunky beak. Darwin asked: Why would God create a different kind of finch for each of these three little islands? He noticed that on each island the food source available was different. On the island with the chunky beaks there were great hard nuts as food. Only a chunky – beaked bird could survive with this food source. On another, there were smaller, more delicate seeds. If you had a wee pointy beak that would be more useful for eating these. Darwin came to this conclusion:

On each island the food source "decided" which birds would survive and which wouldn't. The birds which survived would be the ones who were best suited to the food source on that island. So nature selected which birds would survive and which wouldn't. He called this the theory of Evolution by Natural Selection.

(NB Darwin knew that this happened, but he didn't know how. It was only with the discovery of DNA in the mid-twentieth century that the *mechanism* of evolution became clear).

> ### Task
> Write an imaginary diary entry for Darwin for the day that he realised what his theory really meant.

Pink Pigs and White Pigs

Darwin compared this to animal breeding by farmers. He pointed out that when breeding farm animals, farmers select the features they're looking for in each generation and breed from the animals with the desirable feature only.

Say farmer Giles has only pink pigs. He wants a white one. So he breeds all his pink pigs. Every so often (by random DNA mutation) a pig is born with a wee bit of white. So he breeds the partly white ones only – producing some more white pigs. He then breeds these only. After a while he should have a completely white pig . . . Eventually he can have a stock of white pigs . . .

This is called selective breeding. You breed only those creatures which show the features you want. All Darwin was saying was that nature did the same thing. It "selected" the fittest creatures for any given environment, because only they would survive. The unfit ones (the ones that don't have the really useful DNA for that environment) die out.

Selective breeding

Natural Selection in Practice: The peppered moth

The rise and fall and rise of the peppered moth (*Biston Betularia*) is one of the best-known examples of Natural Selection (even if helped along by human silliness). The peppered moth is speckled grey and white – not unlike the bark of a tree. When the moth lands on tree bark its natural colour disguises it. Birds don't see it so don't eat it. Every now and then a black peppered moth appears (through random

DNA mutation). It lands on the tree (undisguised) and so – hey presto – it is bird breakfast.

During the industrial revolution there was a lot of smoke and soot in the atmosphere. Things were pretty grubby. Trees became covered in sooty deposit, turning them "black". Now, normal coloured peppered moths had a hard time of it. They were now highly visible on the bark and so more regularly eaten. The mutant black ones now had really useful colouring. They were disguised and so not eaten. Before you know it there are hardly any peppered speckled moths left but loads of black ones.

Eventually we humans cleaned up our act and the trees returned to normal. Slowly, but surely the black moths began to get eaten again, and the true peppered moths increased in number.

What would this mean?

Of course, this was pretty shocking stuff in Darwin's day – and scientists and religious people sometimes still argue about it today. This meant that the living things on earth today had *evolved*. Nature had selected them to survive. Many people didn't like this because it meant that God didn't need to be involved in the day to day affairs of nature. In fact, there was no need for a God. This would also explain extinction – evolution was – and is – thought of as "blind". It is simply cause and effect. If the environment changes to suit one species more than another, then that's just tough. The newly unfit species dies out and is replaced by the new improved version.

> **Task**
>
> Design a newspaper front page which covers the peppered moth story.

Humans are just apes

129

Naked Ape?

The problem for most people was that Darwin's theory would also have to apply to humans. Already science was showing close links between humans and other primates. Darwin's theory suggested that humans are just hairless apes who are best suited to the ways things are on earth right now. If this was (is) true, then it means that humans evolved from other living things. It means that they weren't created by God right at the beginning just as they are today. For some people, this was just too much. Humans were special. They had special abilities, above all other living things. This had to point to a creator ... surely? But Darwin's theory suggests not. Humans are one of the end results of nature's blind "choices". Nothing more.

Darwin's Troubles

Darwin really worried about his theory. He seems to have hesitated quite a bit in putting the finishing touches to it. Maybe his wife, who was a very devout Christian, had a part to play in this. She urged him again and again to think carefully about what he was doing. Maybe his own early religious beliefs held him back from what looked like it would be an attack on the Bible, God and the very heart of Christian belief. Maybe he just didn't fancy all the fuss his theory would (and did ... and does) cause.

Historians are still not exactly sure what happened to Darwin's own religious beliefs as a result of his theory. But his own beliefs were definitely shaken not stirred. Before too long the theory of Evolution by Natural Selection was thought of as the one true scientific way to explain the origin and development of life on earth. Even today in the 21st century, it is a brave scientist who challenges evolution.

Darwin was probably troubled by some of the things people might have done (and sadly did) with his theory. "Social Darwinism" was/is the belief that if life is a struggle for survival and only the fittest survive, then it's justified to push the weak out of your way ... that's evolution after all. This is a misunderstanding of Darwin's idea of the "survival of the fittest". The most obvious example of all this is Adolf Hitler's idiocy about the "master race".

The trouble with Evolution?

If it is just a theory then, like all scientific theories, it should be open to challenge. The scientists at the top of the tree (sometimes called the scientific establishment), seem to be a bit annoyed by anyone who attacks evolution. Are they behaving like scientists or "believers" in the evolutionary theory? Usually opposition to evolution takes the following forms:

Evolution is a theory: But some scientists treat it like a religion! Science is about challenging what we just accept. Why should evolution be any different? It should always be open to question.

Evolution isn't perfect: There are some important gaps in the theory. For example, the fossil record does not provide examples of all the possible evolutionary stages which a living organism might have gone through to get where it is today.

Evolution needs guesswork sometimes: We haven't found a complete dinosaur – only bones. Scientists need to make guesses to fill in some of the information like the colour of the dinosaurs or the sounds they made. So is evolution part theory, part belief?

Evolution might tell us how, but not why: If evolution is a "blind" process, then that makes life a fairly depressing thing. It doesn't help us live our lives – in fact it just lowers humans to clever animals. It gives us no real reason to care for others, or strive to make life better . . .

Evolution maybe does away with the need for a God: For religious people, this can't be, because they see evidence of

The 'religion' of Evolution

God in all sorts of other ways. They might say that evolution takes away human hope for a better world – because it's all just too dependent on luck – there's just no point to it. But supporters say that we make our own purpose in life anyway.

The Evidence for Evolution Summarised

◆ Comparing anatomy: Life forms on earth seem to share common features. Some have unused versions of these features (vestigial structures) – like the human appendix. This points to a gradual change or evolution over time

◆ Developing embryos show common features across many species before developing into adulthood

◆ Life cycles show common features (known as the alternation of generations) across species – especially plants. This suggests they are related

◆ Comparing cells and biochemistry: DNA is universal. Almost all cells have the same organelles

◆ Geography: Different species seem to have evolved in different locations. Some species seem to exist only in very small areas and have evolved to cope with very unusual circumstances. For example, thermophiles on the deep ocean floors live only in the super-heated waters produced by volcanism

◆ The fossil record seems to show that through time, organisms become more complex – from the single celled onwards.

Task

From what you have learned so far, do you think the theory of evolution is true?

Your Choice

Scientists who support evolution – and most do – point to the evidence and reasonableness of the theory. But evolution is a scientific theory, not a religious belief. It's not the place of science to worry about what evolution means for human existence. Evolution is a theory. The US National Academy of Sciences describes a theory as;

"A well-substantiated explanation of some aspect of the natural world that can incorporate facts, laws, inferences, and tested hypotheses"

Scientific American: 18 June 2002

The evidence seems to fit the theory well, so scientists accept it as "true". But good scientists know that they should always be

John Burbleblott's solution

on the lookout for a way to improve or question theories. That's how science moves on. Maybe there's a John Burbleblott out there working on it right now.

Source A

At the end of his life, Darwin called himself a theist, a believer in the First Cause. He had doubts though . . . Evolution in no way *implies* atheism, although it is *consistent* with atheism. But evolution is clearly inconsistent with the literal truth of certain revered books. If we believe the Bible was written by people, and not dictated word-for word to a flawless [writer] by the Creator of the Universe . . . then evolution should pose no theological problem. But whether it poses a problem or not, the evidence for evolution . . . is overwhelming.

Carl Sagan & Ann Druyan *Shadows of Forgotten Ancestors* (Arrow books 1993, page 66)

Comments

Carl Sagan was a well-known scientist and atheist. He's arguing here that we have to accept evolution because of the evidence. But he is saying that although evolution seems to do away with the need for a Creator, it doesn't have to be that way. It's only if you try to match evolution up with a literal understanding of the Bible's creation story that you'll have a problem. He points out that Darwin himself believed that God set the whole thing in motion, and that there's nothing to stop someone believing that.

Source B

[My book] seeks to inform, but it also seeks to persuade and . . . inspire . . . I want to persuade the reader, not just that the Darwinian world-view happens to be true, but that it is the only known theory that could, in principle, solve the mystery of our existence. This makes it a doubly satisfying theory. A good case can be made that Darwinism is true, not just on this planet, but all over the universe, wherever life may be found.

From the Preface to Richard Dawkins' The Blind Watchmaker: Why the evidence for evolution reveals a universe without design (Penguin books, 1990)

Comments

Richard Dawkins picks up the argument used by William Paley, about the "watchmaker" (see page 11) of the universe being God. Dawkins suggests that evolution works like a blind watchmaker, having no plan or vision for the future. He argues in his book that evolution points to gradual change brought about by gradual adaptations to the environment, selected by nature just as it happens. He says that looking at the big picture confuses the issue, because each successive change – when you compare it to its predecessor – was simple enough to have happened by chance, but he does see something more here. Dawkins' most unusual suggestion is that living organisms exist for DNA rather than the other way around. This is why another of his famous books is called 'The Selfish Gene'.

- In 1861, a fossil was found. This was the *archaeopteryx*. Some believe that it shows an evolutionary link between reptiles and birds

- It was once said that God must really like beetles. There are around 400,000 species of them!

- The DNA "code" in humans contains about 50,000 – 100,000 genetic instructions

Facts and Figures

Activities

Knowledge and Understanding

Intermediate 1

1 Who came up with the theory of evolution by Natural Selection?

2 How did he come up with this theory?

3 Copy and complete, unscrambling the words underlined.

Eluvonoti is the theory that life on earth began and developed by ceachn. It says that NAD randomly mutates. The change this brings about is sometimes really uulefs. If it is then the living thing with the changed DNA has a better chance of surviving. It also has a better chance of passing on the really useful DNA to its oingffspr. The theory says that life on earth dpedelveo to suit the conditions for life which existed in the environment. So living things are carefully matched to the life they have to live. But this is omnrad and without purpose. It needs no toeCrar. It is ruled by chance. So, Evolution by Natural Selection is ldinb.

4 Copy the statements below, but only the ones which are true. For the ones which are false, find the correct information in the text and write that instead.

- Darwin found the finches on the Sandwich Islands
- In Darwin's day the Christian Church was very powerful
- Geology seemed to show that the earth was only a few hundred years old
- Darwin's theory is called Evolution by Unnatural Selection
- Evolution means survival of the fittest (in a particular set of circumstances)
- The salt moth (Biston Betularia) is an example of evolution
- Evolution doesn't cover the development of human life
- Evolution is a fact
- If you believe in evolution, you can't believe in God

5 In your own words, explain how the John Bubrbleblott story is a bit like the evolution theory.

6 Choose two of the pieces of evidence for evolution on page 132. Explain these in your own words.

7 Read source A again. Does it say that you can't be religious and believe in evolution?

8 Read the comments for Source B again. Explain what Dawkins means by saying that evolution is like a blind watchmaker.

Intermediate 2

1 What is the part played by DNA in evolution?

2 In your own words, describe the evidence Darwin used to back up his theory of evolution.

3 How does the example of the peppered moth support evolution?

4 Why might some people not like evolution being applied to humans?

5 Why might Darwin have been a bit worried about the theory of evolution?

6 Choose two of the arguments against evolution and explain them in your own words. Give your own views on each one.

7 In your opinion, is evolution a theory or a belief? Explain your answer.

8 What does Carl Sagan's quote say about the link between evolution and religious belief?

9 One of Richard Dawkins' books is called *The Selfish Gene*. Read the comments on Source B again. Why do you think his book might be called this?

Practical Activities

1 Carry the Burbleblotts story on. What other possible things could happen? Is it all rosy for the Burbleblotts? Are they invincible? Can anything ever cause their downfall?

2 Using the bullet points on pages 125–126 explaining what Natural Selection is. Draw a cartoon (or some other kind of artwork) to go with each statement.

3 Following a little more research into the adventures of Charles Darwin, write a series of journal entries for Darwin which he might have made during his voyages to the Galapagos Islands. Try to use the kind of language Darwin might have used in his day (you could discuss this with your English teachers). Describe how he comes to realize that the finches on the islands seem to be pointing to something. Describe how he feels as he realizes what his theory of Natural Selection means . . . Here's a start for you.

I must admit to some concern regarding the occurrence of these troubling finches. It would seem, perhaps, that God has made some especial effort to create a distinct bird for each of these unpromising Islands. In truth, I cannot conceive of the Creator's purpose in all this . . .

4 You read this brief letter in a newspaper. You are a scientist who supports evolution. Respond to the letter:

The Editor: Daily Blah
Sir,
I am not related to an ape. I am related to Adam, the first man. I did not develop from single-celled slime. I am the product of a creator God. I am not an accident. My life was planned with a purpose by the Almighty. When will our schools stop teaching this evolutionary silliness?
Yours,
Peter Peterson

5 For each of the following statements, write your own views/responses to the statement – but make it rhyme!

For example:

From single cells we all began; *Does that explain why I'm not a man?*

- DNA is the plan for me
- New life appears from genetic change
- This change happens just by chance
- Darwin thought up evolution
- What does it do to belief in God
- It all started with wee birds
- One good case is the peppered moth
- Means that we're just naked apes
- That explains our vestigial structures
- Nature acts as though it were blind

6 Imagine you've been asked to devise a bill poster which will go on a roadside site. So it has to be very visual and catchy (not too wordy). The poster has been commissioned by the Support Evolution Society in response to people who want to ban the teaching of evolution in schools. Design the poster.

Unit Assessment Question

Intermediate 1: Outcome 3:
"Evolution is the only sensible approach to the origin and development of life on earth". Do you agree? Give two reasons for your answer.

Intermediate 2: Outcome 3:
How far do you agree that evolution is too full of guesswork to be scientifically accurate?

Sample Exam Question

Intermediate 1:
According to Science, how did life on earth begin and develop? (4)

Intermediate 2:
How might some people support their belief that the theory of evolution is wrong? (6)

Homework

Devise a simple crossword on evolution. It should have around five clues down and five clues across.

Funtime

Make a snakes and ladders game based on the evolutionary theory. Go, on, I'm sure it's never been done before! Ladders should be good evidence for the theory. Snakes should be possible flaws in the theory.

The Origin of Life: Christian Belief

Malky is 12. He's been brought up as a Christian. Every Sunday he's enjoyed the Bible stories he hears in Church. Everyone in his Church accepts them completely. Adam and Eve, Noah's Ark, Jonah and the Whale – great stuff.

Malky has also just started secondary school. He's in science. His science teacher is describing the different living things on earth and how they have evolved. Some of it Malky finds confusing. He goes on to talk about humans, and explains they most likely developed from a common ancestor.

Ahah! Malky knows about this. "Sir, Sir" he thrusts his hand into the air. "Yes Malky" replies his science teacher. "That would be Adam and Eve Sir. God made Adam out of mud and breathed life into him. Then he made Eve out of his rib . . . " Malky tailed off because he realised that there was a stony silence in the class. His science teacher cleared this throat a little nervously. Malky was sure a couple of pupils at the back of the class were stifling the giggles. "Thank you Malky", said his science teacher . . . "now, if everyone could turn to page 18 . . . "

Biblical Creationism

What would happen in your school if someone tried to argue in favour of creationism in the science class? Biblical Creationists believe in the literal truth of the Bible story. They argue that God created life on earth as described in Genesis. It's just true. Perhaps that explains the rib-cage differences between men and women?

The story can be accepted simply as a matter of faith. It can't be proved (or disproved). No one was there to see it – except maybe God – so perhaps he told it to the writers of the Bible just as it was. Maybe Adam passed the story on to his children, who passed the story on to theirs and so on. Why not? The Bible is true, therefore so is the account of the creation (so

Spreading Biblical Creationism

Biblical creationists say). Biblical Creationists will not only rely on the truth of the Genesis story, but will point to other places in the Bible where it seems as if the Genesis story is also thought to be true;

"At the beginning of creation God 'made them male and female"

Mark 10:6

These were Jesus' own words. So if the creation story was good enough for him, it should be good enough for all Christians.

Task

How might a Christian reply to the fact that Jesus lived before the theory of evolution was proposed and before the discovery of DNA?

Scientific Creationism

Some Christians don't think it's enough just to rely on the truth of the Bible – especially as there does seem to be a whole lot of evidence for evolution. They look for scientific evidence to show how the theory of evolution might not be as accurate as it seems. They also try to find scientific arguments to support theories like the global Biblical flood experienced by Noah.

What do Scientific Creationists say against the theory of evolution?

◆ Most changes brought about by mutating DNA aren't very helpful. So the idea that DNA mutation produces helpful evolutionary change can't be all that accurate

◆ You can't change what isn't there. Evolution still depends upon there being something there in the first place to evolve from

◆ Why has no scientist shown evolution in action yet? You can

The Origin of Life: Christian Belief

Creating new species

fiddle about with one species till the cows (or should that be dinosaurs) come home, but you can't create a completely new species out of a different one. There are changes within species, but one species has never been shown to become another

◆ The fossil record is incomplete. Why have the fossils of the transitions between species never been found? If evolution is true, we should find the links between, say birds and reptiles – but we don't

◆ The jump between the inorganic and the organic is just too vast to have come about by chance. Living things could not have evolved from non-living things – even over millions of years.

Is belief in evolution a religion?

Scientific Creationists believe that evolution is just one way of interpreting the scientific evidence we have today.

Evolutionary theory is often supported by people who are atheists anyway. Their atheism has come about for different reasons, and it's their starting-point. These people then accept only the evidence which fits in with their atheist views. Science should be open-minded, yet depend on solid evidence. But some scientists who believe in evolution behave more like closed-minded believers in a religion of evolution. They believe in evolution, so they accept the evidence. They don't worry about the problems with the evidence because … they believe in evolution!

Biblically and Scientifically True?

Scientific Creationists also use scientific methods to point to the truth of Biblical events – either to show that they happened, or that they could have happened.

There is evidence for a global flood. The fossil record shows periods of massive extinction, where there's a much greater concentration of extinctions than at other times. The fossil record also shows abrupt changes in living things. If this followed such a flood, then it makes sense that God created living things specially – as they are now. There are plenty of examples of radio (carbon) dating of fossils which point to a very dramatic change in living things around 5000 years ago. This was round about the time that the Bible says that there was such a flood.

> **Task**
>
> Do you think evolution and creation could both be true?

Theistic Evolutionists

Many Christians think that trying to match up evolution and the biblical creation story isn't very helpful. It will mean Christians have to come up with new ways of interpreting new evidence. Christians will always seem as if they're a step behind. They might worry that this makes Christianity look out of touch. The scientific method (see pages 80–81) is very powerful. How can a holy book, written by people from a particular culture, with specific ways of looking at the world, really answer the big scientific questions? If we accept the Adam and Eve story as literally true, then we have to accept all sorts of other things:

◆ that Lot's wife turned into a pillar of salt (Gen 19:26)

◆ that heavenly beings mated with human females and produced giants (Gen 6:1–4)

◆ that Jonah lived inside a large fish (Jonah 1:17)

◆ that Cain's wife was his sister (Gen 4:17)

Theistic Evolutionists believe that Christians must adapt to the findings of science. The Bible is many things, but not a "How I did it" manual written by God to explain the creation of life on earth. It's better if you can blend the findings of evolution together with your Christian faith. There are two ways of doing this:

God the winder-up

The Deists believed that God started the universe off then he didn't interfere again, just like you would wind up an old-

God the winder-up

fashioned clock. So evolution *can* be true because this was what happened to nature after God kick-started it. Some Christians don't like this argument because if it's true, then God is a distant, uninterested figure. There would be no point in prayer because God doesn't get involved. In fact, if it's true, what's the point in believing in God at all – if he doesn't get involved in our lives, then it doesn't matter whether you believe in him or not

Evolution is God's way

Many Christians believe that evolution isn't the opposite of creation, *it's the way God creates*. The real reason behind evolutionary change is not just random responses to changes in

> ### Task
> In your own words, explain why many modern Christians would reject the ideas of Deism.

I think I'll need to try again with this one

Evolution was God's plan

the environment, but God's planned actions. Trouble is, it doesn't explain why God seems to change his mind about the things he makes. But then, if humans are made in his image, why is it so odd that God could change his mind now and again? We do.

It would also help to explain the many similarities between living things. Some creationists wonder, if humans are descended from apes, why are there still apes? The Theistic Evolutionist would answer this by saying that humans didn't descend from apes – apes and humans descended from a common set of ancestors. These branched-off to match different environmental circumstances. There's no reason why a God has to be left out of this – in fact it makes more sense if God is in the equation. After all, who else might be able to cause the massive environmental changes which seem to be the clue to speedy evolutionary changes?

Theistic Evolutionists can also explain why Jesus seemed to support belief in the creation story in Genesis. He was simply being a man of the times. His human self was reflecting the beliefs of the day. Anyway, what would have happened if he had started to tell people the way that God uses evolution as a mechanism for changes to life on earth?!

The big advantage to this approach is that God is still personally involved in everyday life. You can pray to him, because he takes part in life on earth.

What this all means

Some Christians believe in evolution, some don't. But most Christians can still hold on to their beliefs even in the face of the evidence for evolution. As you've seen, they can do this by rejecting the theory or matching it up with their own beliefs. Anyway, their belief in God is usually based on other things.

The Origin of Life: Christian Belief

Source A

www.creationism.org/genesis.htm

The question before you is this: does the fossil record we see today show millions of years this, billions of years that, with almost everything getting buried slowly – or does this fossil record show us evidence of a barely remembered ancient tale of massive global destruction? The old world was destroyed due to sin, according to Genesis. After a horrible re-birth, life on earth began anew. Did this happen about 4,400 years ago (as the Bible teaches) or are we advanced primates with a long illiterate history of swinging from trees, scratching and picking lice off each other, and then for whatever reason (?) inexplicably growing and developing into civilization . . .

Paul Abramson *A Defence of Creationism*

Comments

In this article, Abramson claims that there's plenty of evidence for a flood. He argues that people would be "amazed at just how many holes there are in the evolutionary theory as commonly believed today". He claims that it all comes down to a matter of interpretation based on your starting point. If you begin with the starting point that the Bible story is true, then you can interpret the evidence for evolution vs creation as a creationist just as reasonably as anything else. Evidence has to be understood. This understanding starts from where you are. So Evolutionists and Creationists will understand the evidence differently

Source B

www.cis.org.uk/articles/evolution_relig_signif/alexander_01.htm

As a Christian, I accept the authority of Scripture in all matters relating to faith and conduct, and I believe that the early chapters of Genesis provide us with a theological account of the origins and purposes of humankind . . . . However, I do not personally think that the purpose of the inspired author is to provide us with a scientific account of the origins of biological diversity in general, nor of human origins in particular. Rather the author aims to explain the spiritual meaning and purpose of human existence . . . evolution scientifically provides an explanation, a good explanation I think, for biological diversity – and theologically may simply be viewed as God's way of bringing that biological diversity into being . . .

Dr Denis Alexander, Head of T Cell Laboratory, Babraham Institute, Cambridge: *Does Evolution have any Religious Significance?*

Comments

Dr Alexander argues here that evolution is the way God carries out his acts of creation. Evolution shows us how, but doesn't give us any explanation about why. The Bible is a book designed to explain human purpose in life. It's meant to give us meaning, not scientific explanations.

Facts and Figures

◆ According to some Creationists, the earth is around 10,000 years old: According to science it is over 4 billion years old

◆ Many creationists accept micro-evolution (variations within a type of organism) but don't accept macro-evolution (where one species becomes another)

◆ According to the Bible, Adam lived to be 930 years old. Noah lived for 950 years

Activities

Knowledge and Understanding

Intermediate 1

1 Match this list of statements up with either Ross, Alice or Iain. Ross is a Biblical Creationist, Alice is a Scientific Creationist. Iain believes in Theistic Evolution. Remember, each statement might apply to more than one person:

- The creation story in the Bible is completely true
- If you don't believe in Adam and Eve, how can you believe any of the Bible?
- There are good scientific arguments to support the creation story
- The theory of evolution has lots of gaps in it
- There's evidence for the flood in the fossil record
- God started life off and then let nature take over
- Evolution is God's way of starting and changing life on earth.

2 Copy and complete:

Jesus said, "at the _____ of creation God made them male and female". Many Christians say this shows that Jesus _____ in the truth of the _____ story. Others say that Jesus was just being a ___ of the _____Anyway, if he had tried to explain _____ to the people in his day, they wouldn't have _____.

believed   evolution   Genesis
man   times   beginning
understood

3 Unscramble these sentences to make sense. They are all things a scientific creationist might say against evolution.

- usually helpful mutation isn't DNA
- depends Evolution something being still first on there in the place
- One never species become another shown has been to
- not fossil is The complete record
- evolved Living things things could have from non-living not

4 If we accept the Adam and Eve story as literally true, what other problems could there be with the story of Cain and the story of Jonah ?

5 What would a Deist mean by calling God *the winder-up*?

6 Match up the beginnings of these sentences with the endings:

Beginnings
- If God Just started things off and left them
- Some Theistic Evolutionists say

SCIENCE AND BELIEF

Activities continued

- If you believe in the literal truth of the Bible
- One belief is that Jesus supported the Creation story because he was

Endings
- then it makes him seem uninterested in us.
- sticking up for the importance of the Scriptures.
- that evolution is the way God creates.
- you'll have to explain how Jonah survived inside a fish.

7 Read Source A again. Why do you think the writer has put a (?) in the middle of a sentence?

8 Read the Comments for Source B again. What does Dr Alexander think the Bible is *not* designed to do?

Intermediate 2

1 What do you think might have happened to Malky in your school?

2 What is a Biblical Creationist? Give one reason for their viewpoint.

3 What's the difference between a Scientific Creationist and a Biblical Creationist?

4 In your own words, outline three arguments a Scientific Creationist might use to attack the theory of evolution.

5 Why might some people think belief in evolution is like religious belief?

6 Give one piece of evidence a Scientific Creationist might use to support his belief in Noah's flood.

7 Why might some Christians opt for the Theistic Evolution approach?

8 Why might some people think that being a Deist could be depressing?

9 "Evolution is the way God creates". What does this mean?

10 How might a Theistic Evolutionist explain Jesus' views on Creation?

11 Which part of Source A shows that the writer doubts evolution?

12 Dr Alexander in Source B appears to be a Theistic Evolutionist. What evidence is there in the source to back this conclusion up?

Practical Activities

1 What happens next in the story of Malky? Act this out as a role play in your class. Perhaps you could discuss it with some of your science teachers first. What would they have said/done?

2 Take a pile of blank cards. Sort them into groups of four. Write a statement on each card which represents the views of either a Biblical Creationist, a Scientific Creationist a Theistic Evolutionist (Deist variety) or a Theistic Evolutionist (non-Deist variety). Then mix all the cards up. Pass them to someone else and see if they can put them back into the correct groups.

Practical Activities continued

3 Here is a (fake) question in the Higher Biology exam. In groups of four write an answer for it based on one of the four views in the previous question (one view per answer). You could use your cards to help you now.

Outline and explain the origin of life on earth (10)

Get your teacher to mark it (or better still ask a friendly Biology teacher to mark it!)

4 Have a class debate: "Evolution is the *only* explanation for the origin and development of life on earth"

5 You are a qualified Biology teacher. You have become a Christian in the last year. You now find that you are a Scientific Creationist. You've just applied for a job. At the interview you are asked how you can teach Biology in school while having the creationist views you have. What would you say?

6 Many Christians base their belief in God not on creation (or even the Bible) but on other things. What things could these be? Discuss in class and note your findings.

Unit Assessment Question

Intermediate 1: Outcome 1:
Explain how you can be a Christian but also believe in evolution.

Intermediate 2: Outcome 3:
"Evolution and Creation can't both be true" How far do you agree?

Sample Exam Question

Intermediate 1:
Why do some Christians disagree with the theory of evolution? (4)

Intermediate 2:
Explain what is meant by a Scientific Creationist. (6)

Homework

Write a 50 word (exactly!) answer to this question:

How can you be a Christian and still believe in evolution?

Funtime

The Scientific Creationists Association (don't know if such a thing exists!) has decided to make a short TV commercial outlining its views. Get hold of a video camera and script and act out the commercial. Make it light-hearted.

Does Religion Promote Social Justice? The Challenge of Marxism

If Marx applied for a job, his application form might look like this!

Applicant's Details

Date of Birth: 5 May 1818, in Trier, Germany.

Family background: Jewish family, but my father became a Christian a year before I was born.

Education: I went to a Jesuit grammar school, but I learned more from my very clever father – he was very interested in philosophy and history – so those became my interests too. In 1835 I went to Bonn University, then Berlin University. I did a Doctorate in 1841. It was about Democritus and Epicurus (ancient Greek philosophers).

Employment History: In 1842 I became Editor of a newspaper, Rheinische Zeitung (Rhine Times), but one year later I left due to artistic disagreements with the Prussian Government. I then started up the Neue Rheinsiche Zeitung in 1848. I studied for the rest of my life, and wrote many papers.

Published Works: 1848; The Manifesto of the Communist Party Hundreds of articles for the New York Tribune (and many other publications).1867; Capital, Volume I. Also, many other articles of politics and philosophy.

Hobbies and Interests: Politics, Philosophy, Writing. I have also travelled considerably.

For Office Use only: Comments on application

Unfortunately, Dr Marx died in 1883, so this would make his appointment a little difficult. He certainly was an impressive character as far as the writing was concerned. His works still sell in great number today. More than this, whole societies adopted his teachings and followed his philosophies in every aspect of their daily lives. Many people still think that his views are the best way to run a society for everyone's benefit. However, Dr Marx did find it difficult to hold down a job. He didn't even have a bank account. His views were not welcome by many governments at the time because they were afraid that if people followed them it might lead to revolution. So he was expelled from his homeland (and a few other countries) and ended up living in London.

Although he had an amazing grasp of economics and political philosophy, his own financial skills were rather weak. He spent much of his life quite poor. This poverty also affected his family, who suffered severe ill-health because of it. His educational abilities are obviously good, but he was a bit of a lad at university – even fighting a duel over a woman. He spent most of his time studying and writing. Some might say that this wasn't exactly the real work he wrote so much about. In fact, he died at his desk on 14 March 1883. To think that the royalties from his writings in the years that followed might have made him a very rich man indeed – but would he have wanted that?

> ### Task
>
> Marx has applied to teach politics in your school. Ignoring the fact that he's dead would you give him the job? List the good and bad points about his application.

IT'S A LIVING...

KARL MARX

Marx the teacher

Who was Karl Marx?

Some believe he was a genius – standing up for those who couldn't stand up for themselves. A lot has been said about Marx's own life, and how this shaped his beliefs. Some have used the fact that he was poor and probably neglected his family's needs to criticize his teaching. Anyway, who he was as a person hasn't got very much to do with whether his teachings are right or not. He was just a man – with flaws and weaknesses like everyone else, but the things that he taught certainly got people thinking.

What difference did Marx make?

Some would argue that Marxism has even shaped the history of the world. Marx would like that – because he said that it wasn't enough just to understand history – you had to change it too.

Marx was partly responsible both for the political systems of Communism and Socialism. In Scotland, we have 6 MSPs from the Socialist Worker's Party. Cuba is still a Communist country, as is North Korea. In some countries, particularly in South America, Communism and Socialism are the main opponents of right-wing governments.

Trades Unions are still very common and powerful throughout the world, including here in Britain. Trades unions cover all kinds of jobs – from boilermakers to teachers – and even writers. The idea of a union is to give the individual a power which he or she wouldn't have on their own. Employers are less likely to mess with an entire workforce than with one employee.

What did Marx teach?

Capitalism: Marx said that Capitalists rule the world. These are people who control the means of production. They are the factory owners and landowners and the like. These capitalists live for profit – so that they can get richer. The ordinary people – who Marx called the proletariat (workers) – had to "sell" their labour to the capitalists. Without the Capitalist, you don't have a job – but without you, the capitalist has no one to do the work. So, you need each other. But ... the capitalist has the upper hand – there's always likely to be someone who'll do the work at the rate the capitalist wants to pay. The capitalist wants to do two important things. i. Maximise production – make as much as possible in as little time as possible ii. Minimise costs – make the cost as cheap as possible.

Profit and Surplus Value: Marx called profit "surplus value". This surplus value didn't get back to the workers – it went straight to the capitalist as profit.

> **Task**
>
> On a world map, mark which countries are run by Communist/Socialist or Right-wing governments.

> **Task**
>
> What is the political make-up of Scotland and Britain today. Draw diagrams representing the political parties and the numbers of MSPs and MPs there are from each.

> **Task**
>
> Look at the financial pages of a newspaper or a financial magazine. Find examples of modern-day capitalists. Display these in your class.

For all sorts of things these days you might need to call a helpline. Where the call centre is doesn't really matter – as long as you get the service you're after. So, many call centres are now in places where you can pay people less to work in them. So when you call about your broken TV you're just as likely to speak to someone in Calcutta as in Kirkcaldy. Using cheaper labour means that the profits of the company can be kept high.

Task

What do you think of call centres being moved to the developing world? List the arguments for and against.

The ruling class

De-humanisation: Marx also said that workers were treated so badly that it chipped away at their own identity. Work in Marx's day could be dirty, dangerous and exhausting. Factory jobs were repetitive and mindless. It was quicker and cheaper, but didn't give the worker much of a sense of satisfaction at a job well done.

The Class Struggle: Marx looked at societies throughout history. He noticed that they were usually hierarchical – pyramid-shaped. Once you're at the top you'll do anything you can to stay there. You are then part of the ruling class. The people at the bottom are the working class (the proletariat). The ruling class do what they can to keep the working class in their place, for example, by controlling the means of production, creating levels in society which certain people could never get beyond, or by educating only those who came from the ruling classes. Marx also believed that the ruling classes used religion to keep the proletariat in their place – more of that later. Marx suggested that a fair society was where someone was paid the true value of their labour. But, a capitalist wasn't going to do this out of the goodness of his heart – it was in the capitalist's interest to keep the workers down.

Revolution: Marx wrote: "Workers of the world unite, you have nothing to lose but your chains". He argued that the only way the proletariat could improve their pay and working conditions was to take on the capitalists by uniting against them. The symbol of many socialist groups is a clenched fist. This is because a hand is five individual fingers, but when they unite in a fist, those five fingers become far more powerful. The means of production had to be moved out of private hands and into the hands of the people. The means of production had to be owned by the public. Naturally, Capitalists would not want to give up what they owned voluntarily – so they might have to be forced to by revolution. Marx argued that governments in his day were made up of the ruling classes. The workers needed to unite against the government and overthrow it. Then they could set up their own government based on fairness for all. This would be a government run by the proletariat, not by the ruling classes. Some countries have done this.

The Russian Revolution

How does Marxism Promote Social Justice?

Social Justice can mean many different things – from political power to the right to a fair day's pay. Social Justice is about equality of opportunity. It's about making sure that everyone has the same chances in life. A socially just society is one which is fair. Marx argued that injustices were part of the system which kept some rich and many poor.

Task

What class do you think you are? What reasons do you have for thinking this? How much do you think class matters in your country today? Discuss in your class (!) and note down the ideas raised.

Task

Draw a fist symbol. Explain why it is often used as the symbol of class struggle.

Task

In what ways do you think the idea of revolution could be abused?

Marx argued that the only way to ensure social justice was to take the power away from the few and give it to the many. This would mean re-distributing wealth in society more fairly. By making the rich a little less rich (or a lot less rich) you could make the poor less poor. You could re-distribute wealth by giving land (which had been taken by the state from rich landowners) to the poor. Or, you could take private industry into the control of the state. Any profits which this industry made would go to the government. The government could then use this money to improve education and healthcare – and so society generally would get better for everyone. Marxism can therefore be very practical – a "Robin Hood" approach (taking from the rich to give to the poor) to the way society is ruled.

Marx believed changes in social attitudes were needed. He argued for the rights of women for example. He believed that society should be organised so that real power was in everyone's hands. This is true government by the people.

Putting Marxism into action

Some countries have obviously used Marxist ideas directly, others have used milder forms of socialism. Some have been violent, armed struggles, others have been quiet political changes.

USSR: In 1917, the Bolsheviks seized power from the Russian government. Before this there were clear differences between the lives of the rich and the poor. One of the major figures of this revolution was Lenin. Lenin had studied Marx widely. However, over the years, the new Soviet Socialist government became increasingly isolated from the ordinary people. Many said that it had become just as bad as the Tsarist government and hadn't made life better at all for workers – whose life was still harsh. Socialism here was understood as total control.

Everything was owned by the public (or by the government anyway). There were no private landowners or industrialists. The means of production were controlled by the state. Those who disagreed with the government were treated badly. In the 1980s the USSR collapsed. The Republics broke apart and returned to their pre-revolutionary days. Capitalism has returned – some say with a vengeance. Some argue that the USSR is an example of how Marxism doesn't work. Others don't agree. They say that the USSR's version of Marxism was wrong – not Marxism itself.

Cuba: In 1959, Fidel Castro's revolutionaries defeated the dictator General Batista. Castro took everything under

> **Task**
> Explain, in your own words, what is meant by the redistribution of wealth. How can this be achieved? What is good and bad about it as an idea?

> **Task**
> What examples of social injustice can you think of in society today?

> **Task**
> Look into the history of the collapse of the USSR. Write a short illustrated report about your findings.

Communist Revolution

government control. He used the money from this to ensure that all Cubans had access to free healthcare and free education. Cuba sold much of its produce to the USSR. When it collapsed, Cuba found it harder to survive. Castro is still the leader today (and still very popular). However, the country is moving slowly away from strict Marxist Socialist principles towards a form of Capitalism.

China: In 1949, Mao Zedong became head of the People's Republic of China. He and his Red Army turned China into a Communist state. He became known as Chairman Mao and set up programmes to put Marxism into action. The country became very isolated from the rest of the world. Modern China seems to be moving towards a more capitalist approach as it develops new technology and increases industrialisation.

Socialism and Marxism

In most democratic countries, political groups come from the "right" or the "left". The further you are to the "left" the more you are likely to support Marx's ideas. In the European Parliament there are Communists as well as Socialists. In Britain, the two main parties are still the Labour Party (Left wing) and the Conservative Party (Right wing). In fact, this Labour/Conservative balance is so typical these days that you've probably never known much else – but a Labour government didn't exist in Britain until 1945.

Socialism aims to give power and control to the majority of ordinary people. It tries to make sure that the power in society is widely spread, and not just in the hands of a wealthy few. Socialism in Britain doesn't mean that the government controls everything – and it doesn't mean that you can't get rich. British Socialism simply aims to make sure that the wealth produced by a country is shared fairly among all its members. The NHS is an example of this. Here, the idea is that anyone in Britain can get free healthcare whether they are rich or poor. This puts into practice one of Marx's most famous ideas;

From each according to his ability
To each according to his need

This means that people should give what they can so that others can get what they need. In Britain, this is done through taxes. You pay your income tax according to how much you earn. This pays for things like the NHS and free education.

Criticism of Marx

Marxism doesn't work: Human nature won't let it. Life is a struggle for survival and you take advantage of things where you can. Anyway, once the underdogs get hold of power, they end up being just as bad as the tyrants they have replaced – Stalin and Lenin being perfect examples. Marxism is a very nice theory – but in practice it's not much use.

Marxism cramps your style: Why should people be controlled by the state? Who's to say it knows best? If people aren't free to do what they want, we'll all end up being poor and miserable. Why should everyone be treated the same – people aren't.

I'm not getting up just so I can get exploited

Task

Find out how the NHS is paid for. Find out the two ways you can get healthcare in the USA. Which system do you prefer?

Marxism rewards laziness: Some Capitalists are wealthy because they worked hard. Why should their wealth be taken away from them and given to people who are lazy? Many right-wing critics of Marxism (and Socialism) argue that people should be rewarded for what they do – if they don't then you'll just find people don't put in any effort, or go where their efforts are rewarded.

Revolution: It's a bit of an extreme way to change things, and it can be abused. Sometimes the revolutionaries become the new ruling class – and you're back where you started in the first place.

Good for you Karl

However, supporters of Marx say that Marxism is an ideal, and like all ideals, it is one we should aim for even if we know that we might never get it right. If society was organised so that everyone felt as if they were being treated fairly, then life would be better for all of us, rich and poor. Exploiting others for our own benefit – as Capitalism does – can only lead to problems in the end. Valuing the contribution made by everyone to society is the only sensible way. Marx was a revolutionary in the true sense of the word. He didn't just write about the rights of workers – he also had a strong belief in rights for women and children, who he thought of as being exploited just the same as male workers. Like many important thinkers, supporters say that his teachings were fine, but how people chose to put them into practice wasn't so good.

> ### Task
> What do you think would be good and bad about the government controlling everything?

> ### Task
> If you became part of the government which of Marx's ideas (if any) would you want to try to apply?

> ### Task
> Find examples of where children/women/other groups in society are badly treated today? What steps would you take to try to improve things for these groups?

Source A

The immediate aim of the Communists is the same as that of all the other proletarian parties: formation of the proletariat into a class, overthrow of the bourgois supremacy, conquest of political power by the proletariat . . . In this sense the theory of the Communists may be summed up with the single sentence: Abolition of private property . . . Capital is, therefore, not a personal, it is a social power . . . All that we want to do away with is the miserable character of this appropriation, under which the labourer lives merely to increase capital, and is allowed to live only in so far as the interest of the ruling class requires it . . . Communism deprives no man of the power to appropriate the products of society; all that it does is to deprive him of the power to subjugate the labour of others by means of such appropriation

Karl Marx *Manifesto of the Communist Party* as quoted in *The Marx-Engels Reader* (2nd Edition RC Tucker (Ed) WW Norton & Co.Inc; New York 1972 pp 484–486)

Comments

Marx shows here that he is suggesting overthrow of the political systems which keep the working class proletariat in their "place". He's not calling for a war. Marx calls Capital power, and whoever controls the capital controls the power. He doesn't argue that people should not be able to enjoy the fruits of their hard work – some even take this to mean that he doesn't mind individuals getting a little wealthy if they've worked hard for it – but they shouldn't then use that wealth to keep others down. But Marx is against the ownership of private property – especially where that leads people to get rich at the expense of others.

Source B

Marx saw the essential content of the socialist revolution in the transfer of the means of production from private to public ownership, a process which was to take place under the leadership of the working class as having a greater interest in it than any other class. The question of the form in which this process was to occur – by peaceful or violent means – was for Marx a secondary issue . . . Generally speaking, the older Marx remained faithful to the younger Marx's view that violence is the midwife to every society pregnant with a new one: but he never maintained that violence begets the new society. [Marx himself said that the proletariat would proceed against governments, "by peaceful means where possible, and by force of arms if necessary"]

Ernst Fischer *Marx in his own words* (Penguin Books 1981 pp 131–132)

Comments

Sometimes it looks as if Marx supports violence, other times not. Some Marxist revolutions have been very violent, others have been peaceful. Marx believed that change would not be easy, and that the ruling classes would not give up their benefits easily. But if there was to be justice in society, then they would have to – by persuasion or force.

◆ Three of Marx's children died. He couldn't afford their medicines

◆ Marx remained relatively unknown until Lenin's victory in the Russian Revolution in 1917

◆ In Chairman Mao's China, all party members used to carry around a little red book of Mao's teachings. This was called "The Little Red Book"

Facts and Figures

Activities

Knowledge and Understanding

Intermediate 1

1 Do the following quiz on Marx.

a Date of Birth –
b Religious background –
c Qualifications –
d Edited this newspaper –
e Famous writings –
f Marx's own family problems –
g Date and place of death –

2 Copy and complete:

Some people think ____ was a genius. This was because he stood up for the rights of _____ in his day. He had a difficult life, but he couldn't help it. It wasn't his fault his ideas caused so much _____.
Many believe that Marx has shaped the _____ of the world. The political system of _____ is followed by governments around the world. In Britain, the _____ party is based on socialist ideas.

communism	workers	Marx
disagreement	history	Labour

3 Name two Communist countries.

4 Name one country with a Socialist government.

5 Why would someone think being in a Trades Union is a good idea?

6 Match up the following words with their explanations:

i Capitalist
ii Profit
iii Proletariat
iv Surplus Value
v Capital

a Another word for profit
b The ordinary people – the workers
c The people who control the means of production
d The means of production
e The money "left over" when you take the cost of the product away from the price of the product.

7 Describe one way you could keep labour costs down.

8 What did Marx mean by saying that work could be de-humanising?

9 From the following list choose two ways you could get to be part of the ruling class. Explain how they could lead to you becoming a Capitalist.

i You are born wealthy
ii You are lucky
iii Your parents are wealthy
iv You have a good education

Activities continued

10 Why is a clenched fist often used as the symbol of workers' power?

11 Marx said that Capitalists wouldn't give up what they owned voluntarily. So how did he suggest it could be taken from them?

12 What is meant by the re-distribution of wealth?

13 Choose one of the three countries in this section. Describe how it tried (or tries) to follow Marx's teachings.

14 Name two socialist political parties in the world today from this list

Communists
Socialist Worker's Party
Labour Party
Conservative Party
Liberal Democrats

15 In your own words, describe one criticism of Marx's ideas.

16 Read Source A again. What three things are "the immediate aim of the Communists"?

17 Read Source B again. What did Marx think needed to be transferred from private to public ownership?

Intermediate 2

1 State two things Marx claims about himself in "his job application". Find two things in the "Comment on application" which question these claims.

2 Why might someone feel that Marx himself wasn't working class?

3 How might Marx's own family circumstances lead someone to criticise his teachings? Is this fair?

4 In your own words, describe how Marx's teachings have affected (changed?) world history.

5 In what way is a Trades Union an example of Marxism in action?

6 Explain fully what Marx meant by Capitalism and Capitalists.

7 In what ways could a Capitalist maximise profit?

8 How might a call centre be an example of this?

9 What did Marx mean by "the Class Struggle"?

10 How did Marx suggest that the proletariat could improve their lives?

11 What does Social Justice mean?

12 How did Marx think that the re-distribution of wealth could help promote social justice?

13 Describe how one country has put Marxism into action.

14 In what way might the NHS in Britain be an example of Socialism in action?

15 How might someone argue that Marx's teachings are not the best way to change society?

16 In what ways could you argue that Marx's teaching was ahead of its time?

17 Read Source A again. Is Marx against the idea of the private ownership of property?

18 Read Source B again. Does Marx support violent revolution?

Practical Activities

1 Do some more research on Karl Marx the person. Design and make a short information leaflet on his life. Show some balance in this leaflet – looking at the good and bad aspects of him as a person.

2 Use the internet to find out about trade unions. How many are there in the UK? What jobs do they cover? How are they organised? What do they believe? Report your findings. You could even find out about the range of trade unions in your school. You could interview your school's union representatives – what do they do? What do they see their task as being? How close do they think their trade union is to Marxism?

3 Imagine . . . a Marxist government got into power in Scotland. Write an imaginative essay about how life could/would change for people. Who might benefit? Who might lose out?

4 Write a brief, slightly tongue-in-cheek, instruction leaflet: "How to become a Capitalist".

5 Write a similar tongue-in-cheek instruction leaflet: "How to have a Marxist Revolution"

6 Chrissie is a Marxist, and Chelsey is a Capitalist. They are going to have a debate in your school "Capitalism rules and Marxism is dead". In groups, write the speeches they might have. You could run the debate in your class and then have a class vote at the end.

Unit Assessment Question

Intermediate 1: Outcome 1:
Explain Marx's teachings on the ownership of private property – what might a religious person think about this?

Intermediate 2: Outcome 1:
Explain why a Marxist might argue that revolution is the only way to improve society. How might a religious person respond to this view?

Sample Exam Question

Intermediate 1:
Describe two ways in which Marxism promotes social justice. (4)

Intermediate 2:
"Marxism rewards laziness." To what extent do you agree? (6)

Homework

Private healthcare and education are the opposite of what Marx would have believed in. Devise a list of arguments for and against private healthcare and private education.

Funtime

Marx's ghost comes wandering around Scotland. What would he think? Write a short (humorous) story from Marx's point of view about his feelings about modern Scotland . . .

Does Religion Promote Social Justice? Christian Responses

The first Christians = the first Communists?

All the believers continued together in close fellowship and shared their belongings with one another. They would sell their property and possessions, and distribute the money among all, according to what each one needed.

Acts 2:44–45

The group of believers was one in mind and heart. No one said that any of his belongings was his own, but they all shared with one another everything they had ... There was no one in the group who was in need. Those who owned fields or houses would sell them, bring the money received from the sale, and hand it over to the apostles; and the money was distributed to each one according to his need.

Acts 4:32–35

If anyone has material possessions, and sees his brother in need, but has no pity on him, how can the love of God be in him?

John 1: 3–17

Christian Communism

The first Christians lived lives which could be described as Communism. Many of the very first Christians were wealthy people – many were poor. The rich re-distributed their wealth among their fellow Christians. And yet, there is still some confusion about whether a Christian is allowed to own private property or not. The principle followed by the early Christians was one of simplicity. This would mean that you would have money left over to give away to those who didn't have enough. True Marxism indeed.

All through history there have been rich Christians. Many of the Capitalists Marx complained about – factory owners and the like – would have thought of themselves as good Christians. Most Christian churches on a Sunday in Scotland will have car parks filled with cars, owned by people who have a house, a TV, a DVD player ... should they give it all away? Are they sticking to the example of the "early Christian Communists"? Should Christians be Marxists?

Task

In what ways were the early Christians like Communists? Do you think a Christian should be rich?

Christian beliefs about wealth and poverty

Wealth and poverty are two of the most common topics in the Christian Bible. The general principle is that everything which is needed to enjoy a good life is available – so no one needs to be poor. However, after the Fall, the free meal ticket was taken away. God said that humans would have to work for a living. All their benefits would have to be earned by hard work and the "sweat of their brow". Even so, there came to be very different views within Christianity (and its parent religion, Judaism) about wealth and poverty.

The Old Testament

There are clear strands in the Old Testament about wealth and poverty. However, some of them seem to contradict each other:

◆ *You are allowed to own private property*: In the Ten Commandments, there is one specifically about not being jealous about what your neighbour owns.
"Do not desire a man's house ... or anything else that he owns". Exodus 20:17

◆ *Wealth is a sign of God's blessing*: If you are wealthy and successful in life, then that is because you are "righteous". You have lived according to the law of God and God has rewarded you with plenty. Some Christians today still argue this way. The trouble is that it means that if you're poor, then that is because you are lazy or wicked. Poverty is seen as God's punishment on your wicked ways.
"Be lazy if you want to; sleep on, but you will go hungry". Prov 19:15
"While the lazy man sleeps, poverty will attack him like a robber". Prov 6:10
"Being lazy will make you poor, but hard work will make you rich". Prov 10:4

◆ *Wealth is something you need to be careful about*: If all you're concerned about is getting rich, then you will be blind to the things which really matter in life. Anyway, it's not all it's cracked up to be;

"If you have to choose between a good reputation and great wealth, choose a good reputation". Prov 22:1.

"When you give to the poor, it is like lending to the Lord and the Lord will pay you back". Prov 19:17

A lot of this approach is from books like Proverbs which seems to try to cover all possibilities! A more common way of looking at wealth in the Old Testament is by using the teachings of the Prophets.

◆ *Wealth must be used wisely*: not as something with which you keep the poor down. The Prophets believed that there are many reasons for someone being poor. It could be that they are lazy, or it could be that they've just been unlucky. It might even be God's displeasure. But the human response to it should be a kind and compassionate one. A religious person should try to bring justice to the poor – no matter what has caused their poverty. If you're rich it should be because of your own efforts – not at someone else's expense.
"Doomed is the man who builds his house by injustice and enlarges it by dishonesty; who makes his countrymen work for nothing and does not pay their wages". Jeremiah 22:13
"Evil men live among my people … that is why they are powerful and rich … they do not … show justice to the oppressed". Jeremiah 5:26–28

The prophets believed that the building up and misuse of wealth was an example of people moving away from God. Getting this aspect of life right would mean moving closer to God – and it would also help the poor.

The Teachings of Jesus

Jesus taught that poverty is something which we've got to get rid of because it gets in the way of faith. It also has bad consequences for those who are poor. Just as wealth isn't always good for the wealthy.

◆ *The poor will always be with you* (Mark 14:7): Jesus probably said this to shock people into action – it's a "So, what are you going to do about it then?" statement. It is something which Jesus is saying will always be a feature of life – so it is something we always have to keep an eye on. Jesus himself wasn't entirely working class. He was a skilled craftsman. However, when he began his preaching ministry, he gave this up and accepted a life of poverty. Jesus taught that everyone should be treated fairly and have a chance. No one should suffer needlessly because they are poor.

> **Task**
>
> According to what you have read, does the Old Testament teach that you are allowed to be wealthy?

163

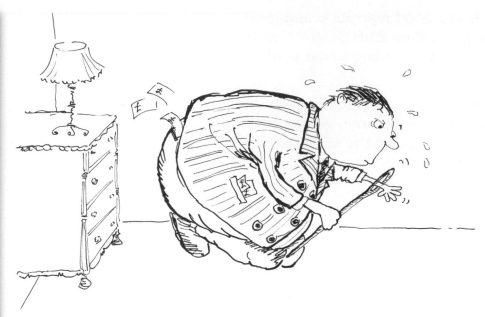

Money isn't everything

Before he taught the crowds he would make sure that they were properly fed. He seems to be saying that there's not much point in preaching to people if you don't care for their physical needs as well. This idea has been picked up particularly by many Christian organisations working with the poor today.

◆ *You must give up all that you own and follow me* (Mark 19:16–30): Christians disagree about this teaching. Some have taken vows of poverty and given away everything they own to the poor. Others have said that Jesus was only warning those who were very rich that they could either spend their lives worrying about money, or use it to help others. So, many Christians believe that being wealthy isn't wrong so long as you have become wealthy by your own efforts and in a fair way. You should then use this wealth to help the poor as much as you can.

◆ *In as much as you do these things to the least of these my brothers and sisters, you do it to me* (Matthew 25:31–46): The teachings of Jesus stressed the idea that everyone was valuable and everyone mattered – whether rich or poor. If you negelected someone or treated them unfairly then it was just like you were doing the same to Jesus. So everything you have comes from God. You must use that wisely for the benefit of all.

> ## Task
> What does Jesus teach about wealth and poverty?

Putting Christian beliefs into action

Most modern Christian Churches and organisations believe that helping the poor is important. They often take two different approaches to this task.

Political Persuasion: Many Christians believe that you have to tackle the causes of poverty. So, you have to get involved in the decisions which split the world into rich and poor.

Direct Action: Poverty is a fact of life. The best way to deal with it is by direct action. This might mean raising money in one country to send to another – or going there to make a difference by helping the poor to help themselves. Two well-known Christian Groups who do this are Christian Aid and CAFOD.

Christian Aid

Its most recent slogan is "We believe in Life before Death". Christian Aid collects money in the UK and uses it to help poorer communities – not only in the developing world, but also here in the UK. It organises charity activities and has a fundraising week every year. Most of its fund-raising activities are done by Christian Churches or organisations here in the UK. On its website it describes itself as;

"An agency of the churches in the UK and Ireland, Christian Aid works wherever the need is greatest, irrespective of religion. It supports local organisations, which are best placed to understand local needs, as well as giving help on the ground through 16 overseas offices."

"Christian Aid believes in strengthening people to find their own solutions to the problems they face. It strives for a new world transformed by an end to poverty and campaigns to change the rules that keep people poor." As far as its work is concerned:

"Out of every pound we receive, 75p is spent on tackling poverty on behalf of the poorest people in the world; 11p is spent on campaigning and education, to change the structures of inequality that keep people poor; 12p is spent on fundraising; 2p is spent on administration.

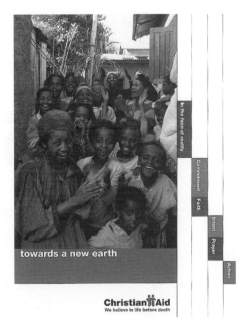

towards a new earth

Christian Aid
We believe in life before death

Funds are channelled into local community groups and church organisations in the countries where we work. These organisations – our partners –

Christian Aid leaflet

165

use the money to help people directly. We do not give money to governments, nor do we fund individuals."

www.christian-aid.org.uk

Christian Aid doesn't have a Bible in one hand and money in the other. It works with partners in each of the countries it is involved in helping the poor. It thinks this is the best way because it means that locals control how the money raised is used. It tends to support whole community projects and doesn't just support individuals. As well as this direct action, it also campaigns here in Britain, to make sure that people are aware of the issues surrounding poverty and injustice. It encourages people to write to MPs, protest about things, and make a difference by supporting Fair Trade organisations. Some have criticised it because some of its work is in places controlled by local partners who are Christian. These Christians might be more likely to help Christian causes than non-Christian ones. However, Christian Aid is aware of this argument and does its best to ensure that the poor are helped, no matter what their beliefs. It is not a missionary organisation.

CAFOD

"CAFOD is a major British charity that has been fighting third world poverty since 1962. We believe that all human beings have a right to dignity and respect and that the world's resources are a gift to be shared by all men and women, whatever their race, nationality or religion."

Its vision statement as stated on its website (www.cafod.org.uk) is;

CAFOD looks forward to a world in which:

◆ the good things of creation are cherished, developed and shared by all;

◆ the rights and dignity of each person are respected, discrimination is ended and all are gathered into a single human family from which no-one is excluded;

◆ the voice of the poor is heard and heeded by all, and lives are no longer dominated by greed;

IT'S TIME FOR JUSTICE

IT'S TIME FOR JUSTICE   CAFOD leaflet

> ### Task
> Write a short report about the work of Christian Aid. How does it put the teachings of the Christian faith into action?

◆ all have access to food, shelter and clean water; to a livelihood, health and education.

CAFOD's work is supported by the Roman Catholic Church and its members. It also works with partners in other countries to make sure that what's needed is what locals decide. Its website covers the wide range of projects which it has been involved in since it began.

Task

In what ways is the work of CAFOD similar to Christian Aid's?

BELIEF AND ACTION

Is Christian Teaching so different from Marx's?

Perhaps the question should really be the other way around. Marx, after all, was brought up in a Christian family, with Jewish ancestors. Although much of the Christian Church at the time of Marx was probably on the side of the rich and powerful, this wasn't entirely true. Many of the great social changes at the time were brought about by Christian individuals and Christian groups. Many Christians, just like Marx, believed that society was unfair. Marx's ideas about revolution – particularly violent revolution would not have gone down well with Christians. Many still believed that the rich and powerful in society were that way because God had chosen them for this purpose.

Many Christians in Marx's day realised that it was a Christian duty to help those in need, and that poverty was something to be got rid of. The re-distribution of wealth was an idea which Christians had practised long before Marx suggested it. Marx's beliefs about equality had already been written about by St Paul

Communism is the same as Christianity

in his letter to the Galatians. Marx's approach to the place of profit over humanity was an old theme from the Bible, the teaching of Jesus and the practice of the early Church.

What's the Difference?

Some Christians have responded to Marxism by saying that Marx only re-emphasised what was original Christian and Biblical teaching anyway. His writings only differ from Christian teachings in that they suggest a practical way to make fairness possible. Christianity and Marxism are both looking for the same outcome. Justice and fairness for all.

> ### Task
>
> From what you have learned so far, list the similarities and differences between Christianity and Marxism in their beliefs about wealth and poverty.

Source A

Is God a Marxist?

Why does scripture declare that God regularly reverses the good fortunes of the rich? Is God engaged in class warfare? Actually [the Bible] never says that God loves the poor more than the rich. But [it does] constantly assert that God lifts up the poor and disadvantaged ... God casts down the wealthy and powerful – precisely because they became wealthy by oppressing the poor of because they failed to feed the hungry ... God does not have class enemies. But he hates and punishes injustice and neglect of the poor. And the rich, if we accept the repeated warnings of Scripture, are frequently guilty of both.

RJ Sider *Rich Christians in an Age of Hunger* (Hodder & Stoughton 1985 pp 64–65)

Comments

Some have argued that God has a "bias" towards the poor. He's on the poor's side. Sider disagrees with this view. He says later in his book that God is impartial. He loves everyone equally, rich and poor. But God does not like the unfairness which comes with wealth and poverty. He doesn't criticise people for being rich, but for getting rich at others' expense – or misusing the power that being rich can bring you.

Source

Capitalism . . . is unashamedly based on the desire to make money . . . It has to be admitted that many Christians seem too often to be compliant in defending activities which promote materialism, individualism and injustice. The problem is that the system of capitalism *demands* a love of money, a desire to maximise profits, and tends to reward those who are most selfish. Indeed it if often argued that capitalism works precisely because people are selfish. The system is said to suit our fallen nature. However, many Biblical writers warn that the kind of pressures which capitalism demands are a challenge to faithful obedience to God. Often they result in exploitation, greed, and injustice.

T Cooper *Green Christianity* (Hodder & Stoughton 1990, pp 84–85)

Comments

Cooper later describes the case of a man lying on a sun-drenched beach. He's asked by a tourist why he's "just lying around". He replies that he's caught all he needs for the day. The rich tourist doesn't understand why he doesn't keep fishing. The he could make more money, own boats, and . . . eventually be able to take a holiday lying on the beach! Cooper argues that the system of Capitalism is linked in with the sinful nature of humans. Christians are guilty of "worshipping" it too. But you can't serve both God and capitalism – both demand different things from you. Cooper suggests that the Christian has to choose which to follow.

Facts and Figures

◆ Tom Monaghan owned Domino's Pizza. He became a multi-millionaire. He's now giving it all away because he believes he'll have more chance of getting into heaven if he's poor

◆ The USA is the world's wealthiest country. Yet Christianity is the most powerful religion there

◆ There are approximately 200 billionaires on Earth. 1 billion people live in poverty

Activities

Knowledge and Understanding

Intermediate 1

1 Copy one sentence in the box on page 161 which shows that the early Christians behaved like Communists.

2 Christians have different beliefs about wealth and poverty. From the list of statements below, put them into one of two columns;

   Evidence that Christians think it's OK to be rich
   Evidence that Christians think it's not OK to be rich

   - Christians today own property like most other people
   - The early Christians distributed their wealth according to people's needs
   - Some Christians own land and some own factories
   - The Ten Commandments say you shouldn't be jealous about what your neighbour owns
   - Wealth is a sign of God's blessing
   - Poverty is the result of laziness
   - Wealth can blind you to the needs of others
   - Jesus said there will always be poor people
   - Jesus said that you must give up everything to follow him
   - Jesus said that it would be very hard for the rich to get into heaven

3 Why might a Christian disagree with the statement "Wealth is a sign of God's blessing"?

4 Was Jesus working class?

5 Copy and complete:

   Jesus taught that _____ and _____ could both get in the way of _____. If you were rich, then that's all you would ____ about. He taught that everything comes from ___,

and so it should be shared fairly. Rich people should be careful because being wealthy would make it hard for them to get into _____. The poor should be helped. When you do this, it's just like you're helping _____ himself.

   **poverty   wealth   Jesus   care
   heaven   faith   God.**

6 How does Christian Aid split up every pound it gets?

7 State three things Christian Aid does.

8 Christian Aid believes in "Life Before Death" what does this mean?

9 Does CAFOD help only Roman Catholics? What evidence do you have for your answer?

10 Copy the true statements from the following list and correct the ones which are false to make them true.

   a Marx was brought up in a Jewish family
   b Many Christians in Marx's day were on the side of the rich and powerful
   c Christians in Marx's day did not care for the poor
   d Christians would always support violent revolution
   e Many Christians in Marx's day saw it as their duty to help those in need
   f The early Christians always kept their wealth to themselves
   g Christians and Marxists should be concerned about poverty

11 Read Source A again. According to this source, does God prefer the poor or the rich? Explain your answer.

12 Read Source B again. Which sentence shows that some Christians support Capitalism?

Activities continued

Intermediate 2

1 What evidence is there in this section that a Christian should support Communism?

2 From what you have learned in this section – should a Christian own property?

3 How might a Christian argue that no-one needs to be poor?

4 What evidence is there in the Bible to show that poverty is caused by laziness? What problems might a Christian have with this teaching?

5 Why does the Bible also teach that you have to be "careful about" wealth?

6 Find one quote in this section which suggests that wealth should not come from the exploitation of others.

7 Jesus said that the poor will always be here. Does that mean a Christian should just accept the existence of poverty? Explain your answer.

8 Why do some Christians think Jesus taught that you should become poor?

9 How does Christian Aid raise and spend its money?

10 What criticisms are sometimes made about the work of Christian Aid? How does Christian Aid respond to these criticisms?

11 Organisations like CAFOD don't only raise money and give it to the poor – they also campaign to get people thinking about poverty. Do you think they should spend their time doing this? Explain your answer.

12 Which of the Christian teachings in this section do you think could have influenced Marx's beliefs?

13 What similarities and differences are there between Marxism and Christian teaching about wealth and poverty?

14 Read Source A again. What evidence is there in the passage to show that God is unbiased?

15 Read Source B again. According to Cooper, why are Capitalism and Christianity likely to be in conflict?

Practical Activities

1 Here is a (fictitious) letter written to a Christian magazine. Write the response you might make to it. Post your responses on a display board in your class room.

Dear Sir

As a Christian, I'm fed up being told that I shouldn't have money. I work hard for the money I earn. Why shouldn't I enjoy it? All around I see so-called poor people getting handouts from the government, and then spending the money on drink, satellite dishes and fancy holidays. I'm careful about what I spend and invest it wisely.

Isn't it about time somebody stood up for the rich? After all, God helps those who help themselves.

2 Design an information leaflet which could be given to a local Christian Church. (Maybe once it's finished you could!). This leaflet is to explain Christian teaching about wealth and poverty. You should look at the Biblical teachings as well as the examples of Christian Churches and organisations. Can a Christian be rich? What should a Christian do about the poor?

Practical Activities continued

3 Look at the websites for CAFOD and Christian Aid. Use the information there to prepare a display board on their activities. What are their current campaigns and projects? How do they raise and spend their money?

4 Write an imaginary dialogue between a Christian and Karl Marx which starts with the Christian accusing Marx of stealing all his ideas from Christianity.

5 Write a discussion between two Christians. One believes that wealth is a sign of God's blessing, whereas the other thinks that the wealthy should be ashamed to call themselves Christians.

6 Look at some of the Bible quotes in this section on the issue of wealth. Choose one and make it the basis for a piece of artwork. This could be a drawing, painting, or even something like a sculpture using everyday objects.

Unit Assessment Question

Intermediate 1: Outcome 3:
Marx's teaching about social justice is just the same as Christian teaching" Do you agree? Give two reasons for your answer.

Intermediate 2: Outcome 1:
Why should Christians be concerned about the poor?

Sample Exam Question

Intermediate 1:
Explain how a Christian could help make the world a fairer place. (4)

Intermediate 2:
"The similarities between Marxism and Christianity are greater than the differences". How far is this statement accurate? (10)

Homework

Look up the Christian Organisation TearFund. In what way is it similar to/different from Christian Aid and CAFOD?

Funtime

Marx and Jesus meet in heaven (!), how might their conversation go?

Is God Real or Imagined?
The Challenge of Marxism

The real God

Will the real God please stand up?

For Marx, like many in his day who began to look at religion in
a critical way, it was obvious that the idea of God was a little
confused. There was God the kindly old gentleman pointing
out his gardening work in Eden. But there was also the God
who helped the Israelites destroy cities. There was also the God
who didn't take kindly to being ignored, and who killed almost
everyone in a flood to prove it – except the chosen few. There
was God the bully, picking mercilessly on Job. There was a
God with a strange sense of humour who persuaded Abraham
to put the fear of death into his son by almost sacrificing him.
There was the God who had a taste for the burnt flesh of
animals. Finally of course, there was the God who sacrificed his
own son to pay a debt owed . . . to himself.

This kind of confusion led many in Marx's day to question the
whole idea of God. This was especially true of those who were
puzzled by what they saw as the gap between the religion of

173

Christianity and the Church which seemed to side with the powerful. It was a time when many religious revivals took place – urging people to go back to an earlier, purer form of Christianity.

Marx believed that religion was just one stage in human development. This development should lead eventually to humans being their own "gods".

God the Projection

Marx was a fan of the philosopher Ludwig Feuerbach.

Feuerbach was a materialist. He believed that existence is completely physical – all thinking and knowing come from the physical processes in the mind. The only way that we can know anything is by investigation leading to evidence leading to proof. The material universe is all there is. This is the opposite of Dualism – which says that reality can be split into two things – physical bits and spiritual bits. Dualists argue that all thinking and knowing come from the spiritual bits. Feuerbach's Materialism led him to believe that God is just something inside our heads. We make him up in our minds. This means he has no existence outside of our heads. Feuerbach pointed out that the God of the Old Testament wasn't all that different to a human;

> Thus in ancient Judaism, Jehovah was a being differing from the human individual in nothing but the duration of his existence, in his qualities, his inherent nature, he was entirely similar to man – had the same human passions, the same human, nay, even [bodily] properties ...

Essence of Christianity, Part II,
Chapter XX The False or theological Essence of Religion

It therefore seemed to Feuerbach that it was more likely that man made God in his own image than that God made man in his. The Bible was written by humans who made God seem human-like. He argued that if God was what religious people claimed, then he was so unique that he could only be understood in a

God is a projection

Task

In your own words, explain why the character of God could seem to be a little confused.

BELIEF AND ACTION

unique way, using unique techniques. This didn't make much sense.

Feuerbach thought of God as a projection of human wishes. Feuerbach meant that we make God what we want him to be. He said that;

> The fundamental dogmas of Christianity are realised wishes of the heart – the essence of Christianity is the essence of human feeling.

> *Essence of Christianity Part I, Chapter XXIII The True or Anthropological Essence of Religion*

So, he argued that Jesus was the ultimate in wish-fulfilment, because;

> To see God is the highest wish, the highest triumph of the heart … Hence, only in Christ is the last wish of religion realised, the mystery of religious feeling solved … for what God is in essence, that Christ is in actual appearance …

> *Essence of Christianity Part I, Chapter XXIII The True or Anthropological Essence of Religion*

Feuerbach really said that we want there to be a God so we project one "out there" so we can believe in him. The real historical Jesus just hit the spot as far as human wish fulfilment was concerned. Up to then God was remote and abstract – with Jesus he was here and personal. According to Christians Jesus was "God made flesh". Feuerbach saw this as a weakness – Jesus was just the fantasy of God come to life.

> ### Task
> What's the difference vetween materialism and dualism? Which view do you think is right?

> ### Task
> Why might Jesus be the "ultimate in wish-fulfilment"?

Marx on Feuerbach

Marx argued that people were the product of circumstances and upbringing. Marx wanted to argue that humans are active, not passive. We can change our circumstances and improve them. He thought Feuerbach was right – religion was made by humans to satisfy their own needs. But he argued that we can't just leave it there;

> Thus, for instance, after the earthly family is discovered to be the secret of the holy family, the former must then itself be criticised in theory and revolutionised in practice.

> *Theses on Feuerbach. Thesis IV (1845)*

Marx meant that it wasn't enough just to explain religion away as something which was all in the mind – we have to look at what this means for human life. One of Marx's most famous statements is made at the end of his Theses on Feuerbach – and this is not surprising. Marx believed that the wish-fulfilment which was religion tended to keep people living in a fantasy world. Marx urged people to stop dreaming and take practical control to change things for the better;

> The philosophers have only *interpreted* the world, in various ways; the point, however, is to *change* it.

> *Theses on Feuerbach, Thesis XI* (1845)

Marx on Religion

Marx argued that what we saw in religion was what we wanted to see;

> Man, who has found in the fantastic reality of heaven, where he sought a supernatural being, only his own reflection, will no longer be tempted to find only the semblance of himself – a non-human being – where he seeks and must seek his true reality.

> The basis of irreligious criticism is this: man makes religion; religion does not make man

Contribution to the Critique of Hegel's Philosophy of Right (1843)

Marx goes on to make probably his most famous comments about religion. He argues that religion is an illusion which people cling to because their lives are so miserable. He wants to abolish the need for religion, by improving society so it's no longer necessary;

> The abolition of religion as the *illusory* happiness of men, is a demand for their *real* happiness. The call to abandon their illusions about their condition is a *call to abandon a condition which requires illusions*. The criticism of religion is, therefore, *the embryonic criticism of this vale of tears* of which religion is the *halo*.

Contribution to the Critique of Hegel's Philosophy of Right (1843)

He argues that the very existence of religion is something which keeps people numb to their circumstances, and importantly, holds them back from doing anything about it;

> Religion is the sigh of the oppressed creature, the sentiment of a heartless world, and the soul of soulless conditions. It is the opium of the people.

Contribution to the Critique of Hegel's Philosophy of Right (1843)

Opium was a popular drug in Marx's day. It had the effect of giving you a sense of happiness which disappeared as soon as the drug wore off. But it also made you dopey and unable to do very much except lie around and look goofy. It was obvious that Marx meant religion had the same effect. You couldn't change the world if you were spaced out – whether on drugs or on the fantasy of religious belief.

The abuse of religion

Marx argued that the ruling classes used Christian beliefs and practice as a way of keeping people in the "rightful place". This was done in at least two ways;

He said that religion was used to make people accept their poor situation in life. The Christianity of Marx's day tended to teach that you should accept your "lot" in life, because God would reward you in the afterlife. This meant that people didn't put as much effort into improving their lives as they probably should have. Marx argued that the Christian Church used this to make sure people didn't get restless and think of doing anything rash, like overthrowing the ruling classes. Also, it would be wrong for you to complain about your conditions, because the ruling classes were put there by God to rule. The fact that they were rich and you were poor was because they were righteous and you weren't. Marx argued that the church's teaching was obvious; if you went against the wealthy, you were going against God.

The Christian Church in Marx's day was still very hierarchical. There were even churches where there were luxurious padded

Accept your position in society

177

seats for the wealthy (with lockable access to them!) and hard, uncomfortable seats for the less well-off. The Christian Church was still very socially unmixed. The established Church in Marx's day was still seen by many as being on the side of the rich and powerful – supporting the capitalists, not the proletariat. Remember too, that most ordinary people couldn't read or write – so they depended upon those in charge of the Churches to explain to them what the Bible taught – and so what God wanted – as far as social behaviour was concerned.

Task

Why did Marx criticise Christianity in his day? Do you think his complaints still apply to Christianity today?

Positive Humanism

Marx didn't want just to stop at the criticism of religion. Again, he thought that people had done this in the past but it hadn't changed anything. He thought it was just a negative approach to the whole question of the human condition. It wasn't enough just to say there was no God – Marx wanted to suggest what to replace this lack of God with. For him, that was Communism leading to positive humanism. His argument was that only once humans became fully aware of their own power to change things would life get better. Marx thought that religion, atheism, and even communism were just stops along the way towards mankind's final goal – total self-reliance. Humans would only succeed in life by taking control and making the world the way they wanted it to be. Maybe Marx would have been chuffed with the mantra of the 21st century – "Just Do It!".

"Modern" Marxism and religion

Strangely enough, wherever Marxism and Communism took hold, there was and still is, an uneasy relationship between the Communist state and religion.

◆ *The USSR*: After the Russian Revolution, Atheism became the "state religion". Christianity was banned and churches were closed down or destroyed. However, all through the history of the USSR, the Christian faith survived. Though persecuted, it managed to stay alive – often meeting in secret, knowing that its followers could face hard punishments. Christians like Alexander Solzhenitsen kept their faith alive and kept the world's attention on the plight of Christians in Communist USSR. When the Soviet Empire collapsed, Christianity returned. Churches re-opened, priests came out of hiding, Bibles were printed and read openly again.

◆ *Cuba*: In this still-Communist state, religion is still practised openly. Roman Catholicism is strong here, as well as religions which have their origins in Africa, brought to Cuba

A Russian Orthodox Church

by those who were slaves. The statistics show this; today in Cuba, the split of beliefs is 44.1% Christian, 30.9% Atheist, 25% Spiritist. In 1990, Fidel Castro met with leaders of Christian Churches. He changed the law to allow Christians to become members of the Communist Party, and even to become members of the government. Castro even met with Pope John Paul II in 1998.

◆ *China*: There are disagreements about how the Christian faith is treated in China. Some argue that it is tolerated, but others accuse the Chinese government of persecution. The government has tended to leave Christianity alone as long as Christians don't try too hard to make converts. But, as Christianity is a missionary religion, this sometimes leads to

Fidel Castro meeting Pope John Paul II in 1998

conflict. The Chinese government sometimes argues that it is not attacking Christianity, it is just against the Western culture which sometimes comes with it. It sees this as a threat to the Chinese way of life and so something to be resisted.

Did Marx or Christianity win?

Maybe this isn't the right question. Marx argued that religion was imagination. Where Marxism has been put into practice, religion has always remained. Today, the relationship between Marxism and Christianity seems less strained. Perhaps Marxists have decided that Christians aren't always on the side of the rich and powerful – or perhaps Christians have decided that Marx was dead right about lots of the practical things. It is probably true that Christianity today is not the weapon of the ruling classes, but something which puts the needs of the poor first. It probably encourages social change. So perhaps Christianity and Marxism don't need to be on opposite sides at all.

> ### Task
>
> In your own words, explain how Christianity has been treated in these three Communist states.

Source A

Man makes religion; religion does not make man. Religion is indeed man's self-consciousness and self-awareness so long as he has not found himself or lost himself again. But man is not an abstract being, squatting outside the world. Man is the human world, the state, society. The abolition of religion as the illusory happiness of men, is a demand for their real happiness. The call to abandon their illusions about their condition is a call to abandon a condition which requires illusions.

Karl Marx, *Contribution to the Critique of Hegel's Philosophy of Right* as quoted in *The Marx-Engels Reader (2nd Edition)*, RC Tucker (Ed) (WW Norton & Co. Inc, New York, 1972 p 54)

Comments

He's saying that religion is something which humans have created to help them make sense of the difficult world in which they live. He argues elsewhere that religion is a stage on man's development towards Communism. It served a purpose at one time, but is no longer needed. All it does is keep people in their place, by offering them fantasies to replace the horrors of their daily life. Marx was arguing that if daily life were improved for ordinary people, then they wouldn't need religion any more – they could "quit the habit".

Source B

The belief in revelation exhibits in the clearest manner the characteristic illusion of the religious consciousness . . . man can of himself know nothing of God; all his knowledge is merely vain, earthly, human. But God is a superhuman being; God is known only by himself. Thus we know nothing beyond what God reveals to us . . . the divine revelation is determined by the human nature . . . the contents of the divine revelation are of human origin . . . for they have proceeded directly from human reason and human wants. And so in revelation, man goes out of himself, in order . . . to return to himself! Here we have a striking confirmation . . . the knowledge of God is nothing else than a knowledge of man!

Ludwig Feuerbach, *Essence of Christianity: Part II, The False, or Theological Essence of Religion,* Chapter XX1

Comments

Feuerbach argues that the revelation of God was very common in the past, but now seems less obvious. As a materialist, he wants solid objective proof for beliefs, but according to him, this isn't usually what you get. So, you just have to believe. Now this belief is just your own thinking. If God existed, he would be such a powerful being that you couldn't possibly understand him anyway. So you make him up according to what you can understand. But, for Feuerbach, this is the only place where God is – your own creation inside your own mind.

- ◆ Marx wrote some romantic poetry in his youth
- ◆ There are estimated to be around 50 million Christians in China
- ◆ Fidel Castro is the longest-serving political leader in the world today

Facts and Figures

Activities

Knowledge and Understanding

Intermediate 1

1 Give one example from the first section of why someone might think God's character was confused.

2 Match the beginning of the sentence with the ending:

Beginnings
a   Marx was a fan . . .
b   Feuerbach was a . . .
c   Materialism is the . . .
d   Dualism says that . . .
e   So for a materialist . . .
f   Feuerbach said that man . . .
g   So Feuerbach said that God . . .

Endings
i   materialist.
ii   reality can be split into physical and spiritual bits.
iii   God is all in your (physical) head.
iv   of Ludwig Feuerbach.
v   made God.
vi   is a projection, just wish-fulfilment.
vii   idea that reality can only be explained by physical things.

3 What did Marx mean when he said, "The philosophers have only interpreted the world . . . "?

4 Why did Marx want to abolish religion?

5 Copy and complete, re-ordering the words/phrases underlined;

Marx argued that religion was often used as a improving their conditions The ruling classes used it to keep people the ruling classes had been chosen by God to rule. The poor would get their reward for their miserable lives in rulers. Marx said the Church kept people from rising up against their heaven. Anyway, many Christians at the time taught that in their place. So if you

went against them you went against God. So Christianity in Marx's day kept people from rocking the boat and social tool.

6 Do this quiz:

a   What did Marx mean by Positive Humanism?
i   Taking control of your own life
ii   Depending upon God
iii   Just being an atheist.

b   After the Russian Revolution;
i   Christianity became the state religion
ii   Atheism became the state religion
iii   The Church became the state religion

c   In Cuba:
i   Most people are atheists
ii   Most people are Christians
iii   Most people are Spiritists

d   The Chinese government has;
i   Banned Christianity
ii   Tolerated Christianity
ii   Fought Christianity

7 From what you have learned about Marxism and Christianity so far, do you think they are opposites? Explain your answer.

8 Read Source A and the comments again. When does Marx think people could eventually "give up" religion (or "quit the habit")?

9 Read Source B and the comments again. According to Feuerbach, where is God?

Intermediate 2

1 From your reading of the first part of this chapter, what two possible arguments might someone in Marx's day have used to question the existence of God? How fair do you think these arguments are?

Activities continued

2 What did Feuerbach mean by saying that God is a projection? What do you think?

3 Explain the difference between materialism and dualism.

4 Explain one argument Feuerbach used to support his idea that man made God in his own image.

5 In what way might Freud and Feuerbach be linked?

6 Explain Feuerbach's idea that Jesus is the ultimate in wish-fulfilment.

7 Why did Marx think Feuerbach hadn't gone far enough?

8 What did Marx want to do about religion? Explain why.

9 In what ways did the Christian Church in Marx's day possibly help Marx's arguments against Christianity?

10 Explain why Marx thought "Positive Humanism" was better than religion.

11 Using the three Communist states in this chapter, what evidence is there to show that Marxist Communism hasn't "beaten" Christianity?

12 Read Source A again. Why does Marx think that religion doesn't lead to "real happiness"?

13 Read Source B again. What did Feuerbach mean by saying that the "knowledge of God is nothing else than a knowledge of man!"?

Practical Activities

1 Choose one of the characteristics of God in the Bible (either positive or negative). Draw your own cartoon to illustrate this. Display these in your classroom under a heading; "Will the real God please stand up?".

2 Write as many reasons as you can to explain why people might "want to believe in God".

3 Imagine you are interviewing Marx about his views on Feuerbach. You want to know why he thought Feuerbach was right, but you also want to find out how Marx wanted to improve upon Feuerbach's ideas. Write the dialogue which might result from your interview. You could act this out in class, or record it if you like.

4 If you wanted to change the world today – what things would you do? Discuss this in groups and report back to your class. How different is what you want to do from what might have been needed in Marx's day?

5 Imagine you are a rich Christian in Marx's day who is also a factory owner. You are trying to persuade your workers to accept their (pretty horrible) conditions because they'll get their reward in heaven. Either; write the speech you might make to them along these lines or; design a leaflet to hand out to them. Remember – most of your workers will only be able to read a little (or not at all).

6 Choose one of the Communist States in this chapter (or another you're interested in). Carry out a mini-project into it using the following structure:

- History of this country
- How it became Communist
- How it put/puts its Communism into action
- The relationship its leaders had/have with religion/Christianity
- How closely it stuck/sticks to Marx's ideas about religion

Unit Assessment Question

Intermediate 1: Outcome 1:
What did Marx mean when he said that religion was the "opium of the people"?

Intermediate 2: Outcome 3:
Marx taught that religion makes people accept their poor conditions. How far do you agree that this is true?

Sample Exam Question

Intermediate 1:
Explain what Marx meant by saying that belief in God was an illusion. (4)

Intermediate 2:
Explain why Marx thought religion should be abolished. (6)

Homework

Imagine you had to write a set of "Commandments" for the new "religion" of Positive Humanism. What would those Commandments be?

Funtime

Marx and Fidel Castro meet. After discussing the problems of having beards, they go on to discuss Communism. Write the dialogue.

Is God Real or Imagined?
Christian Responses

Will the real Donald please stand up?

So God has more than one aspect to his personality – so what? Who doesn't? That doesn't make us all dangerous psychopaths lurking down dark alleys. According to Christians, God is not confused about his personality – he's just like us in that he has different 'faces' for different situations. Take, for example, Donald.

Donald is a powerful businessman. He's in charge of hundreds of people.
Donald is a Dad. He has to act responsibly for his children.
Donald is a swim coach. He is relaxed yet firm here.
Donald is a son. His Mum can still make him feel small.
Donald is a customer in shops. He gets easily embarrassed when trying on trousers.
Donald has just joined the gym. He feels a bit pathetic next to the guys with bulging biceps.
Donald is a holidaymaker. You should see what he wears to the beach. Just as well none of his employees can see him!

Donald's just doing what's normal – being different 'people' at different times. Christians believe that God is the same. In different circumstances he behaved in different ways. Does that make him an imaginary figure?

> **Task**
> How many "faces" do you have?

God is real

How might a religious person argue that God is real, not just imagined?

◆ *The Argument from Design*: The universe and everything in it seems just right for its purpose. Christians argue that this wasn't just pure chance, but the thought-out actions of a creator God. It's just too much to accept that everything just happened instead of didn't happen, so there must be something which made it happen. This leads to ...

185

◆ *The First Cause argument:* Everything needs a cause, including the universe. But unless the causes go back forever, and that doesn't make much sense according to Christians, there has to have been a first cause which caused all the rest. The only thing which could possibly be that very first cause is God.

◆ *The Argument from Religious Experience:* Many people have experienced God, directly, or as a guiding force in their lives. Some of these experiences are fairly dramatic, others are quiet and subtle. Whatever it's like, the result is usually the same – the person changes for the better. This change can then be used as 'evidence' to prove that God is real, and not imagined. We'll come back to this . . .

Feuerbach and Marx: Contradictions and leaps of logic?

Number 1

Feuerbach and Marx took a very scientific approach to life. Proof had to be solid and real. The existence of a spiritual world was rejected. Materialism was king – everything was physical. So God must be a physical thought in your head. But. This argument has a few wee holes in it because, like Christianity, it starts from an already held belief and then moves from there to "prove" that this belief is right.
So, what Feuerbach said was this;

a. I don't believe in a spiritual dimension to life

b. So there must be physical proof of the existence of God.

c. I can't find any (that I'm willing to accept)

d. So God doesn't exist (except in your imagination)

e. But I can't prove that God is a spiritual force

f. Because . . .

Number 2

Feuerbach believed that God was a projection of human wishes. This belief of his proved to him that God doesn't exist. But how can you jump from the *belief* that God is only a projection to the *physical truth* that God is only a projection?

Suppose I have in my hand a tin with no label. Without being able to open the tin (or X-ray it or something), I can never know what's inside it. But more than that, I can imagine it's full of beans, or custard, or tiny little universes filled with strange tartan monsters. Now the truth is, that any one of these is a possibility and, whatever I *imagine* is inside has absolutely no effect whatsoever on what is *actually* inside.

Feuerbach and Marx both jumped from the *belief* that God is imaginary to the *fact* that God is imaginary. Is that completely fair?

Number 3

Both Feuerbach and Marx (and later, Freud) argued that God is wish-fulfilment – imaginary. Imagine that I wish for a paradise island where the rivers are made of chocolate and there's an endless supply of everything you could ever want. I could wish this all day every day. Would the fact that I'm wishing it change whether it was real or not? It was once said, "Just because I'm paranoid doesn't mean they're not out to get me". Every person who ever lived could wish that there was a God and that would still have absolutely no effect on whether there actually is a God or not.

Some Christians might argue that Feuerbach and Marx both ended up where they started – at the beliefs they already had for one reason or another. So in fact, they weren't being materialists at all – they were just replacing one set of beliefs with another.

Belief or fact – do you know what's inside?

> **Task**
>
> In your own words, explain why believing that something is true or false *doesn't make it* true or false.

> **Task**
>
> Do you agree that Feuerbach and Marx have just replaced one "religion" with another? Explain your opinion.

Imagine there's no heaven …

Marx argued that religion was a drug. Even if it was (or is) – what's the problem? Christians would argue that most of us need propped up at some point in our lives. We might get this support from friends, family, our colleagues at work, or God. Does our need for this kind of support mean that those who give it to us are less likely to exist than if we didn't need them? Your friend exists whether you need her or not. Her

existence doesn't depend on your need. So, God's existence doesn't depend on your need either. And what about heaven?

But for many people, belief in justice for everyone after death was (and still is) something which helps them through their lives and gives their lives great meaning. Christians might argue that it gives you a lot of hope. Does Communism give you the same? Some Christians would go further and argue that believing there's no heaven, or judgement after death, makes you more likely to abuse and exploit people in this life. The Christian belief in the afterlife means that you will have to face the music for your bad deeds ... eventually. Such a belief should make you want to treat people fairly.

How much proof did Marx and Feuerbach need?

Many Christians will simply point to those whose lives have been changed for the better by their faith. Why isn't this enough proof that there is a God? Christians would point to the effectiveness of individual Christians, organisations and Churches throughout history and still today, to support their belief that God is real because he makes great things happen. If the proof of a belief is how effective it has been in making the world a better place, then sadly for Marx, Communism hasn't done too well ...

9 out of 10 people prefer religion

Many Christians will argue that Marx's views on religion have been shown to be weak because people have stuck to religion

Judgement after death

Task

List three things you think would be good about there being a heaven and three things which might be bad about it.

Task

In what ways do you think Communism offers people hope?

Task

Do you think people's dramatically changed lives are enough proof that God is real? Give reasons for your answer.

where they have rejected Communism. The fall of the USSR is the most obvious example. Now that Communism has collapsed, Christianity is taking off like a rocket in the former USSR. This is proof that Marxism can't replace Christianity. They could even argue that in some Communist countries, Communism just became a new religion.

In the USSR, it was common for ridiculously larger than life statues of Lenin and Stalin to be erected all over the place. Huge paintings of revolutionary heroes became ... objects of worship? Now, of course, Marx probably wouldn't have approved of all that, but it maybe suggests that Marxism was lacking something which it needed to make it really work – a mischievous Christian might suggest that something was God.

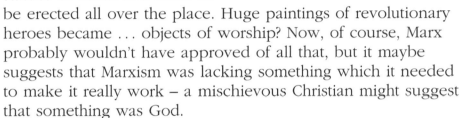

Humans prefer it . . .

Changed days

Christians today might agree that Marx had a point about the Christian Church in his day. It probably was used by the rich and powerful to keep the proletariat in their place. But is it still like this? Most Christians would admit that there's still a bit of that side of Christianity in the world today, but far, far less than in Marx's day. However, even in Marx's day, organisations like the Salvation Army were suggesting that Christians should do more to help the poor. But they weren't just suggesting it, they were doing it. It set up homes for the poor and tried to help them improve their own lives. It went out into the streets and helped those in need. It still does. The Salvation Army was founded in London in 1865 when Marx was 47. At this time Marx was living in ... London.

So Christians were then, and are now, in the front line in the fight against poverty, injustice and unfairness. Christians have been, and are, active in politics and governments throughout the world to make the world a fairer place. Christians believe that their work on earth is bringing about the Kingdom of God. They're trying to make the world the kind of place which God would want it to be. This is very practical – not just offering empty hope. In fact Christians could argue that they're not just

Task

Why do you think Christianity survived throughout the Communist era in the USSR? Give as many reasons as you can.

Task

Look up the Salvation Army's website www.salvationarmy.org.uk. Write a page on what it does today and why it does it.

The Salvation Army taking action

helping people improve their lives now, they're helping them prepare too for their life to come with God. Many Christians would argue that Christianity has done far more to make the world better than Communism ever has, and if that isn't solid proof that God is real, what is?

Positive Christianity

Marx's positive Humanism was a way to take control of your life. He suggested that religion encouraged you to do nothing about life's nasties. You either waited for God to do it, or just put up with things until you died – then everything would be hunky-dory. Christians would argue that their faith is very positive. It's a get up and do faith, not a sit back and don't. Even in Marx's day, one common saying was that "God helps those who help themselves". This meant that you had to be active in your life to make your life better. You shouldn't just wait for God to put it right for you.

Christians today put this into practice. They believe in helping the poor and the oppressed, in justice and in equality. They also argue that their belief in God gives their life meaning. What they do has a purpose. They take action and do things to make people's lives more meaningful – both physically and spiritually. For Christians, their beliefs give them hope. Not just hope that this life will get better, but that they will eventually get a fair deal from God. God's justice will lead to everyone getting exactly what they deserve. A God who they say isn't just in your head, but exists in reality too.

> ### Task
> State one way in which Christianity is like Marxism, and one way in which Christianity goes further than Marxism.

Source A

What about the Christian Socialism of FD Maurice, Charles Kingsley and JM Ludlow in mid nineteenth century England? Was that not an attempt to apply the Christian gospel to the condition of the working class in 1848 and to create a Christian alternative to revolution? What about the social gospel of Walter Rauschenbusch … in America in the later part of the nineteenth century? Was that not an attempt to realise … the Kingdom of God on earth and to implement Christian teaching about the 'brotherhood of man' in the world of business and politics. What about the more radical teaching of the religious socialists in Switzerland and Germany around 1900 who influenced the young Karl Barth to the point of proclaiming that socialism was a predicate of the gospel?

Brian Hebbelethwaite, *Christian Social Ethics in a Global Context in Ethics in the World's Religions* (J Runzo & NM Martin (Eds) Oneworld 2001 p 310)

Comments

In this book, Hebblethwaite tackles the argument that Christianity doesn't have much to say about social issues. He mentions the Christian teacher Karl Barth who argued for a form of Christian Socialism. But Hebblethwaite argues that Christianity goes further than Socialism because Christianity isn't just concerned with people's rights because of its belief in "natural law and human dignity", but because of the example of Jesus, and the desire to make the Kingdom of God a reality here on earth, now.

Source B

This generation has grown up ignorant of the fact that socialism is as old as the human race. When civilization dawned upon the world, primitive man was living his rude Communistic life, sharing all things in common with every member of the tribe. Later when the race lived in villages, man, the communist, moved about among the communal flocks and herds on communal land. The peoples who have carved their names most deeply on the tables of human story all set out on their conquering career as communists, and their downward path begins with the day when they finally turned away from it and began to gather personal possessions. When the old civilizations were putrefying, the still small voice of Jesus the Communist stole over the earth like a soft refreshing breeze carrying healing wherever it went.

I have said, both in writing and from the platform many times, that the impetus which drove me first into the Labour movement, and the inspiration which has carried me on in it, has been derived more from the teachings of Jesus of Nazareth than from all other sources combined.

James Keir Hardie *From Serfdom to Socialism* (1907)

Comments

James Keir Hardie was born in Lanarkshire in 1856. He was born into poverty and ended up working in the mines. However, his mother taught him to read and, to cut a long story short, in 1892 he became Britain's first Socialist MP. Although he was brought up as an atheist, he became a Christian in 1897. He began to argue that Christianity and Socialism weren't so different. He became the first ever leader of the Labour party. These quotes show that for him, Christianity and Socialism shared the same social ideals.

◆ One of the friends of James Keir Hardie, the Christian Socialist, was the atheist Eleanor Marx. She was Karl Marx's youngest daughter

◆ Worldwide, the Salvation Army runs 800 hostels for the poor, 2100 food distribution centres and 202 Children's homes

◆ In a recent poll in the UK, 76% of respondents said they believe in some form of life after death

Facts and Figures

Activities

Knowledge and Understanding

Intermediate 1

1 How does the character of "Donald" help us understand God?

2 Match the information below with the correct argument for the existence of God

   a   The Argument from Design
   b   The First Cause argument
   c   The Argument from Religious Experience

   i   This says that everything in the universe seems just right for its task. It can only have been created by a God which made it fit for its purpose.
   ii   This says that something which happens to you points to there being a God. Maybe it changes you dramatically for the better.
   iii   This says that everything needs to have started seomwhere. So God must have been the thing which started it all off.

3 Copy and complete.

Feuerbach argued that there was no _____ dimension to life. This meant that there would have to be _____ proof of God. But Feuerbach couldn't find any. But if God is a spiritual _____ then there won't be any physical _____. Feuerbach doesn't believe in spiritual things __ so he can't _____ (or disprove) there's a God.

     physical   proof   spiritual
         prove   being

4 What does it mean to say that Marx and Feuerbach jumped from the *belief* that God is imaginary to the *fact* that God is imaginary? What do you think?

5 How might a Christian argue that believing in heaven isn't a bad thing?

6 Do you think Communism has failed? Give a reason for your answer.

7 Give one reason why some people think of Communism as a religion.

8 What do you think Marx might have thought of the Salvation Army?

9 Christians might argue that some people might want to believe that God is imaginary. Why might someone want to do this?

10 What evidence might a Christian give to "prove" that God isn't just in their heads?

11 Read Source A and the Comments again. What did Karl Barth argue for?

12 Read Source B again. What was James Keir Hardie's "inspiration"?

Intermediate 2

1 How could you argue that the "many faces" of God don't harm belief in him?

Activities continued

2 In your own words, explain what is meant by the Argument from Design, the First Cause argument and the Argument from Religious Experience. Do you think these prove that God is real?

3 How does Feuerbach's view that everything has a physical explanation lead him to believing there's no God? Is he contradicting himself?

4 What's the link between the tin with no label and belief in God on page 187?

5 Does wishing for something make any difference? Explain your answer in relation to belief in God.

6 Were Feuerbach and Marx just replacing one religion with another?

7 Why do you think Feuerbach and Marx were rejecting religious experience?

8 Has the collapse of the USSR proved that Marxism is a failure? Explain your answer.

9 Did the USSR turn Communism into a religion?

10 Do you think the Salvation Army behaved in a way that Marx would have liked? Explain your answer.

11 How might a Christian argue that Christian Actions have shown that God is more than a figment of your imagination?

12 In your opinion, what are the similarities and differences between Christianity and Marxism?

13 Read Source A again. What do you think Christian Socialism is?

14 Read Source B again. How does Keir Hardie argue that Socialism "is as old as the human race"?

Practical Activities

1 Take four or five sheets of A4 paper. Staple them together like a booklet. On each page, write about one of your "faces". Perhaps you could write about you the son/daughter or you the friend etc. Show how each "you" is different.

2 Take arguments numbers 1–3 on pages 186–187. Imagine Feuerbach and Marx could reply to these criticisms. What might they say?

3 Have a class debate;
"This house believes that Christianity gives you hope while Communism makes you hopeless."

4 Find out about the state of Christianity and Communism in the world today. Prepare a sheet of Facts and Figures showing how many people follow each one etc.

5 In a magazine, the following letter has been written. Write a reply which could be made by a Christian putting the opposite argument.

Dear Sir,

Christianity is a disease. Marxists should beware! It teaches pie in the sky when you die. It's still used in the 21st century to keep the proletariat down – imagine! It teaches about a fantasy figure called God – but it lets the same old abuses of the people happen. Never mind – it'll be OK when you get to heaven. Hah! Follow Marx – he's the one who can truly satisfy. Christians sing, "God be in my head" – just as well, that's the only place he is . . .

6 Christians believe that their faith gives their life meaning. Discuss in groups how this might be true. Make notes about what you decide. How else can people find meaning in their life if they don't have religious beliefs?

Unit Assessment Question

Intermediate 1: Outcome 1:
How might a Christian argue that their work for the poor in the world shows that God is real?

Intermediate 2: Outcome 2:
Marx argued that religion was the 'opium of the people'. How might a Christian respond to this?

Sample Exam Question

Intermediate 1:
"Belief in God makes life meaningful" Do you agree? Give two reasons for your answer. (4)

Intermediate 2:
How far do you agree with Ludwig Feuerbach that God exists only in your mind? (6)

Homework

In 100 words answer the following question:

"Believing in heaven gives your life meaning"

Write a tongue-in-cheek article for a teenage magazine:

"Ten reasons why Christianity is better than Marxism"

Oppression and Liberation: The Marxist Approach

The oppressed proletariat

Christmas? Bah Humbug!

Ebenezer Scrooge wasn't far off the mark as far as many employers in Marx's day were concerned. Many workers had only a day or two off work every year – and only then because these were holy days – hence holidays. In Marx's day, anyone could be put to work. People of any age, women, children. In fact, women and children were far more likely than men to be taken advantage of because of their "weak" position" in society. In general, working people were exploited. They worked hard, but were paid little. As well as this economic oppression, people were oppressed in other ways too. Oppression simply means keeping people down – keeping them powerless and unable to change their lives for the better. If you're worked hard and paid miserably, then it's obvious you're being oppressed, but there were other ways of oppressing people:

◆ Education was expensive – so only the rich could afford it. If you had no education it meant you had fewer chances in life.

BELIEF AND ACTION

◆ Healthcare – in Marx's day, there was no free healthcare. If you were ill you had to pay for medical treatment – or heal yourself. Even buying medicines was beyond many people (remember, this was probably why two of Marx's own children died). If you are in poor health, then you are less fit to work, and so you get poorer. A very vicious circle.

◆ People were also oppressed in less obvious ways. There was a very rigid class system in Marx's day. It didn't do you any good to get "ideas above your station". This meant that if you were poor and working class, then you would always be thought of by the ruling classes that way – no matter how much you "bettered" yourself. All areas of society were strictly run according to class – from Church to Government.

All in all, there were many ways in which the poor were kept poor. A common saying of the poor at the time went like this:

"God bless the squire and his relation and keep us in our proper station." In other words, don't rock the social boat. Accept your life and your place in the pecking order and get on with it.

What's changed?

Some would say that the poor are still kept poor, but in more subtle ways. Let's compare;

◆ There's still a thriving private education system in Britain. This can only be afforded by a few. Does it give you a better education? Some argue that it gives you status – having gone to a private school helps you get on in life.

Task
Discuss: Do you think there's still a class system in Britain? What evidence do you have for your opinion?

Task
Do you think people should try to "better" themselves? How can this be done?

Modern-day social exclusion in Britain

They argue that most of the top professional jobs in Britain are still done by people who had a private education. Now too, if you want to go to university, you have to take out loans to pay for it. This means that students from wealthy families can concentrate on their studies, but those from poorer backgrounds might have to take on part-time jobs to help pay their way through the system.

◆ In Britain, healthcare is free – almost. Dental treatment isn't and you still have to pay for prescriptions. People can pay for private care if they can afford it. This might mean that how good your healthcare is still depends on how wealthy you are.

◆ Politics is open to everyone now – but it might be worth asking just how many MPs and MSPs come from wealthy backgrounds. How many had private education? How many paid for their university education? Whether or not there's still a class system in Britain is a subject people argue about even today. But still some argue that there's a "glass ceiling" of social class in Britain. You can progress so far up the social ladder, but there comes a point where you are stopped because you don't have the "right" accent or come from the "right" background.

Changing World

Comparing the worker's lot at the time of Marx to today only gives us part of the picture. Yes, there's still exploitation of workers and all the oppression which goes with it. There are still sweat shops and people who are in a kind of slavery to

> ### Task
> What evidence can you find to suggest that people are just as oppressed today as they were in Marx's day? You could design a collage for your room comparing then and now.

Oppression and exploitation in the Third World

pay off their debts – even in our own country. But there are also lots of laws about working practices which weren't around in Marx's day. There's also lots of support and help for the poor.

But this isn't true everywhere in the world. In the developing world, oppression and exploitation can be every bit as bad as it was when Marx was alive. Child labour is still very common. There are still people who are poorly paid, working in dirty dangerous jobs, and being taken advantage of at every opportunity. There are people who can't afford healthcare, who are excluded from choosing their own governments, who have no access to education. It looks as if the world which Marx knew is still alive and unwell in the developing world.

Rich World, Poor World

Sometimes people are oppressed in the developing world by their employers. This is the same old capitalist greed. Sometimes it's the government which oppresses the people – but even they can't always help it. Many developing countries owe lots of money to the developed world. Their governments have to pay this back. This means they have to make their people work hard to get the money to do this. The people work, but don't get the benefit.

Sometimes the developed world sets up business in the developing world. Companies can pay the workers there less, and they don't have to worry so much about looking after the workers because the laws about how employers treat workers aren't as strict as they are in the developed world. This means that the companies can do just what the employers in Marx's day did. Keep production costs down (by exploiting the workers) and so maximise profits.

Trouble at 't mill

As you can imagine, this can easily lead to people wanting to rise up against the rich and powerful and take control themselves. In the developing world there's usually a small ruling class, powerful, educated, wealthy. They also often control the governments – which usually means controlling the forces of law and order too – like the police and the military. They then use these things to keep the oppressed in their place. All this could lead to more instability in the world. Economic refugees are becoming a big issue in the developed world, sometimes ending up in tension between communities.

Task

Do a search on the internet under the headings "child labour" and "modern slavery". What examples are there of oppression of people in the world today?

Task

Find out about the kinds of rights workers have in the UK today.

Marxist Revolutionaries

Sometimes, where people have found that they are being oppressed, they've had revolutions. This often means that they have had armed struggles against ruling governments. There have usually been popular leaders who have been able to organise the ordinary people into fighting forces.

Ernesto 'Che' Guevara (1928–1967)

Che Guevara

Guevara studied medicine in Argentina. He became horrified at the poverty he saw in his home country and throughout Latin America. He began to think that the only way to help people out of their poverty was through violent revolution. He helped Fidel Castro overthrow the dictator Batista in Cuba. He became part of the government and travelled the world helping other socialist revolutionaries. In 1967 he was shot in Bolivia while helping train revolutionaries.

Guevara believed that Capitalism had taken on a new form – colonialism. It was reaching out around the world to take control away from the people. For Guevara, the USA was the worst example of this, perched as it was towering over tiny Cuba. Guevara was convinced that the only real way to change the lives of the poor for the better was through armed revolution:

> "We can not and may not cherish the illusion that we can obtain freedom without battle. These battles won't be restricted to streetfights with rocks and teargas, nor will they be peaceful general strikes, nor will it be the battle of a furious nation that in two or three days will have destroyed the repression apparatus of the ruling financial oligarchy. This battle means a long war, and I repeat it once more, a cruel war ..."

> "Hate will be an element of the battle, a merciless hate for the enemy, that will inspire the guerrilla-soldier to

superhuman efforts of strength and changes him into an effective, violent, selected, in cold blood killing machine. That is how our soldiers must be; a nation without hate can not triumph over a brute enemy."

www.el-comandante.com

Fidel Castro (1927–)

Fidel Castro

The longest serving political leader in the world is still in his post today. Castro too believed in the need to overthrow the ruling class – if necessary by violent struggle. However, he tried to oppose the military dictatorship of Fulgencia Batsita by peaceful means. He tried to use the legal system as he was a highly qualified lawyer. But this failed and he ended up building a revolutionary force in Mexico which eventually overthrew the Batista government. Once he became leader, he took privately owned industry into government hands.

Although Castro used violent struggle to seize power, some think that he has mellowed in his old age, and is no longer so keen on the use of violence as a way of getting power for the people. Of course, some don't agree with this, and see him as an old-fashioned revolutionary supporting violent struggle around the world. Compared to Che Guevara's fairly aggressive tone, Castro's is much softer. After the revolution, many wondered what would happen to those who had fought against him and his forces. Castro's answer was this:

> However, I will repeat here what I have already said, "and history will absolve me," that we shall insure that maintenance, assistance, and education shall not be lacking for the children of the military who died fighting against us because they are not to blame for the errors of the tyrant. We shall be generous to everyone because, as I have said before, here there are no vanquished, but only victors. The war criminals will all be punished because it is the irrevocable duty of the Revolution to do so and the people can be certain that we shall fulfil that duty. The people

should also be sure that when justice reigns there will be no revenge because if on the morrow there are to be no assaults made against anyone, justice must reign now. Since there will be justice, there will be no revenge nor will there be hatred.

Castro, *Things will be the way people want them:*
www.marxists.org

Task

What do you think are the good and bad points about Guevara's and Castro's way of living out their Marxist beliefs?

Some are more equal than others

In 1943, George Orwell wrote a book called *Animal Farm*. In it the pigs lead the rest of the animals on the farm into a struggle against their human masters. But by the end of the book a strange thing has happened. The pigs have become the new masters – every bit as bad as the old human ones. In fact, the very last paragraph of the book states:

> No question, now, what had happened to the faces of the pigs. The creatures outside looked from pig to man, and from man to pig, and from pig to man again; but already it was impossible to say which was which.

George Orwell *Animal Farm* (Penguin Books 1984 p 120)

This is one of the major arguments against Marx's ideas about freeing people from oppression by revolution. Power has a habit of corrupting people. Once the people become powerful and control their own lives, they fall into all the same old traps that the people they replaced had fallen into. Some would say that this is what happened in the USSR. The leaders of the people just became the new oppressors of the people. Perhaps

Animal Farm

Oppression and Liberation: The Marxist Approach

Marx's idea that violent struggle was the only way to achieve change was flawed. Maybe power, no matter whose hands it is in, corrupts the people who wield it.

Maybe too, violent struggle doesn't work because it just leads to an endless cycle of revenge. Maybe persuasion is better than force. Maybe violent struggle is just too open to being abused. However, many supporters of Marx still believe that when all else fails it might be the only way.

Source A

Someday the worker must seize political power in order to build up the new organization of labour; he must overthrow the old politics which sustain the old institutions, if he is not to lose heaven on earth like the old Christians who neglected and despised politics. But we have not asserted that the ways to achieve that goal are everywhere the same ... and we do not deny that there are countries ... where the workers can achieve their goal by peaceful means. That being the case, we must also recognise the fact that in most countries on the Continent [of Europe] the lever of our revolution must be force; it is force to which we must someday appeal in order to erect the rule of the labour.

Karl Marx *The Possibility of Non-Violent Revolution* (1872 in The Marx-Engels Reader; WW Norton, 1978 p 523)

Comments

Did Marx suggest that violent revolution was the best or only way? Obviously not. He argued quite clearly that in some situations peaceful revolution could achieve the goals of Communism. When the political system allowed it, people could non-violently choose a communist system and assure, in his own words, "world domination by the proletariat". This could only happen where there was democracy to start with. In cases where there were dictators in power, this would obviously be more difficult. Marxists today still disagree about whether violent struggle is the right option or not.

Source B

It is sheer mockery of the working and exploited people to speak of pure democracy, of democracy in general, of equality, freedom and universal rights when the workers and all working people are ill-fed, ill-clad, ruined and worn out not only as a result of capitalist wage-slavery, but as a consequence of four years of predatory war, while the capitalists and profiteers remain in possession of the "property" usurped by them and the "ready-made" apparatus of state power. This is tantamount to trampling on the basic truths of Marxism which has taught the workers: you must take advantage of bourgeois democracy which, compared with feudalism, represents a great historical advance, but not for one minute must you forget the bourgeois character of this "democracy", its historically conditional and limited character. Never share the "superstitious belief" in the "state" and never forget that the state even in the most democratic republic, and not only in a monarchy, is simply a machine for the suppression of one class by another

From V. I. Lenin *Collected Works, 4th English Edition,* (Progress Publishers, Moscow, 1966 Vol. 28, p 370)

Comments

Lenin was one of the founding fathers of the Russian revolution. Here he argues that democracy can sometimes be another form of dictatorship. It can sometimes work only for the capitalist against the proletariat. It can be just as much in need of overthrowing as the royal dictatorship which was the Tsar in Russia. This kind of view is why Marxists often oppose even democratically elected governments and seek to overthrow them. It's not enough for the Marxist to say that a government has been elected by the people – because often such governments end up seeing to the needs of only a small minority in society – the rich and powerful.

Facts and Figures

- In 19th century textile factories, the youngest children were used as scavengers. They had to pick up loose bits of cotton from under heavy pressing machines – while the machines were running

- In Thailand today, 240,000 to 410,000 children, or 2–4% of children between the ages of 6–14, work in urban employment. (US Dept of State Human rights report 1998)

- In a poll on the Internet in November 2002, 32% of respondants reckon Fidel Castro will still be in power in 10 years time (see www.pollit.com)

Activities

Knowledge and Understanding

Intermediate 1

1 Copy and complete;

In _____ day, workers had almost no _____. Almost anyone could be made to work, including _____. You were worked hard and weren't_____ very much. You didn't even have many _____. This is called _____ and is one kind of _____.

> exploitation   rights   holidays
>   children   paid   oppression
>   Marx's

2 The following are ways people were oppressed in Marx's day. Match the form of oppression to its explanation.

    a Lack of education
    b Poor (or no) healthcare
    c Strict class system
    d Economic exploitation

    i   If you were working class you would always remain that way in the eyes of the ruling class. You'd probably never get into certain positions of power in society.
    ii If you got sick and needed medicine you had to pay for it. But while you were ill and couldn't work you didn't get paid.
    iii You had to pay for education. Without it, you'd find it hard to "better" yourself.
    iv As a worker you didn't have many rights. There weren't many rules about the health and safety of workers which employers had to follow.

3 In Marx's day, only the wealthy could get an education. Give one reason why some people might argue that it's gone back to being like that today.

4 Do you think people are better off nowadays than in Marx's day? Give one reason for your answer.

5 What is a sweatshop?

6 What is bonded labour?

7 What does "Power to the People!" mean?

8 Copy and complete re-ordering the underlined words:

When people are <u>instability</u>, they will be angry about their lives. They might want to <u>ruling classes</u> up against the rich and powerful. Marx said they should <u>power</u>. But the <u>rise</u> sometimes use the forces of <u>law</u> and order to hold on to their <u>revolt</u>. All this oppression and revolution could lead to more <u>oppressed</u> in the world.

9 What did Che Guevara think people would have to do to improve their lives?

10 Why do you think some Marxists would not agree with Guevara's way of doing things?

11 Read the quote by Castro on page 200 and the quote by Guevara on page 199. Find one difference in their views.

12 Match the beginnings of these sentences with their endings:

Beginnings
    a In *Animal Farm*, the oppressed
    b So after revolutions maybe the new leaders
    c Some say this is exactly what happened
    d Maybe violent struggle just leads to.
    e Marxists though, believe that revolution gives people back the

Endings
    i   in the USSR.
    ii become the oppressors.
    iii endless acts of revenge.
    iv power which has been taken from them.
    v just become the new oppressors.

Activities continued

13 Read Source A and the comments again. Which sentence possibly shows that Marx agreed with violent revolution?

14 Read Source B and the comments again. What does Lenin say about democracy?

Intermediate 2

1 Explain, in your own words, how workers in Marx's day were oppressed.

2 What other kinds of social oppression were there in Marx's day?

3 What does the quote "God bless the squire and his relation, and keep us in our proper station" mean?

4 What do you think are the similarities and differences between oppression in the UK today and in Marx's day?

5 Why do you think someone today might just put up with exploitation and oppression?

6 Do you think there is any exploitative child-labour in Britain today?

7 How might the debts of the developing world lead to the exploitation of people there?

8 How might a developed world business exploit (or take advantage of) developing world workers?

9 Why might oppression lead to revolution?

10 What form of revolution did Guevara argue for?

11 Why did he think hate was needed in a revolution?

12 How did Castro end up as Cuba's leader?

13 What are the similarities and differences between Castro and Guevara?

14 How might someone argue that *Animal Farm* is an example of the problem with revolution?

15 What possible drawbacks are there with violent revolution?

16 How might someone use the USSR as an example of the problem with revolution?

17 Read Source A again. Was Marx for or against the use of violence in revolution?

18 Read Source B again. How does Lenin criticise democracy?

Practical Activities

1 The story, *A Christmas Carol*, by Dickens is an attack on the oppression of the poor and a satire of the rich and powerful. Discuss this book in class – what examples are there in it of exploitation and oppression? Write a brief report of your discussions.

2 Design a poster using a collage of images; "The Class system in Britain today."

3 Try to find out about your MPs and MSPs. You could use sources such as "Who's Who?." How many of them had private education? How many of them went to University etc.? How many of them would you describe as "working class"?

4 What makes someone one class and not another? Discuss your ideas in groups and then write out the "requirements" for being; Working Class; Middle Class; Upper Class. (If you want you could extend this to look at lower middle class and upper middle class etc.)

5 Design a poster: Rich World, Poor World. This could compare wealth in the developed or developing world – or between the two.

6 Imagine you thought a revolution was necessary in the UK today. How would you go about it? Draw up your plans!

Unit Assessment Question

Intermediate 1: Outcome 1:
What was Marx's solution to oppression?

Intermediate 2: Outcome 3:
"Marx's advice to the oppressed is unhelpful" How far do you agree?

Sample Exam Question

Intermediate 1:
What advice does Marx give to the victims of oppression? (4)

Intermediate 2:
How far do you agree that the Marxist response to oppression and exploitation does not work in practice? (10)

Homework

Find out about modern Cuba. In what ways does it still follow Marx's teachings? In what ways has it changed its beliefs to match the needs of the modern world?

Funtime

A TV game show offers a million pounds to anyone who is working class if they can pass themselves off as upper class for a week. Write an imaginative story based on this idea.

Oppression and Liberation: Christian Approaches

4.4 billion people live in developing countries. Of these;

◆ Three fifths lack basic sanitation

◆ Almost one third have no access to clean water

◆ A quarter do not have adequate housing

◆ A fifth have no access to modern health services

◆ A fifth do not have adequate protein and energy from their food supplies

www.cafod.org.uk

What is Poverty?

The Catholic Aid organisation, CAFOD, says that poverty is,

> "More than a lack of what is necessary for materials well-being, poverty can also mean the denial of opportunities and choices most basic to human development – to lead to a long, healthy creative life; to have a decent standard of living."

Poverty isn't just lack of material wealth it's having no choices in life – no hope and no sense that the future will improve. Christians are also bothered about the effects of poverty. Many people don't get their fair share because others are greedy and take more than their fair share. The Christian view of oppression isn't that different to Marx's view. It is denying a person the chance to make their life better – keeping them in their place in many different ways. Also, has poverty really changed in the 21st century? There are still workplaces around the world today of which the Capitalists from Marx's day would be proud.

The causes of poverty in the developing world – where almost all the world's most serious poverty is today are:

◆ *Globalisation*: Companies seek out the cheapest resources and labour around the world. They can pay those in the developing world less

◆ *Debt*: Developing world countries have borrowed from the developed world. They have to work to pay this back

◆ *Trading*: Developing world countries don't have the same economic power as the developed world. If the developed world chooses not to buy your produce – or fixes the price, there's nothing you can do

◆ *Land Use*: Much land in the developing world is taken away from the people and used by foreign-owned big-businesses

◆ *Corrupt government*: In many developing world countries, the government sides with the rich developed world for its own benefit, or for the benefit of a wealthy few in that country.

> **Task**
>
> Design a poster collage of images which represent the division between Rich and Poor in the world today.

Christians and Communists – friend or foe?

So you'd think Christians and Communists would team up more often wouldn't you? If they both agree that oppression is a bad thing, and that you need to take action to end it, then surely they could agree to work together – so why haven't they?

Since the beginning of Marx's Communism, there has been mistrust between some Christians and some Marxists. Marxists see Christians as helping to keep the oppressed in their place by offering them a false hope that things will get better. Is this fair?

◆ Many Christians do believe that governments and rulers are chosen by God. This means that they should be obeyed

◆ There is a long tradition in Christianity of the Church supporting rulers. Sometimes this was just sensible – having a ruler as an enemy wasn't seen as a very good idea – and getting the ruler to become Christian could mean the whole nation becoming followers

◆ On the other hand, the Christian Church has opposed rulers and governments where they have been cruel or unfair

◆ There have always been individual Christians prepared to oppose unjust rulers – sometimes they have died for their beliefs.

> **Task**
>
> Discuss: Do you think that Christians should support the government all the time?

But there is still this mistrust. The Catholic Theologian, Dom Helder Camara summed this up perfectly;

"When I fed the poor they called me a saint. When I asked, 'Why are they poor?' they called me a Communist"

Dom Helder Camara

There's always been this tension in Christianity. Pretty much all Christians agree that it is a Christian's duty to help the poor in practical ways. But there's disagreement within Christianity about how much Christians should get into politics and start asking questions about the reasons why so many people are poor. Some Christians have decided that Christianity and Marxism aren't so very different in their beliefs about oppression and the need to deal with it. This has been most obvious in the area of Liberation Theology.

Option for the Poor

Liberation Theology began in the 1960s in Latin America. It started with Roman Catholic priests who were working and living in poor communities. They started to notice the difference between the sometimes airy-fairy teaching of the Church and the real day to day needs of the poor. They realised that before someone could understand and accept the gospel, they should be freed from the grinding misery of their poverty-stricken lives. Individual priests began to argue that Christian beliefs should be worked out in action, or *praxis*. They believed that Christianity should make the poor more powerful, not just in a "it'll all be sorted out in heaven" sort of way, but in a real and practical way here and now. They began to talk about Liberation Theology. Liberation in this sense meant;

◆ Working out your beliefs for yourself in relation to your own situation – not having them imposed from "above"

◆ Freeing yourself from poverty, injustice, oppression

◆ Freeing yourself from the effects of sin and returning to God and your fellow man.

Liberation Theologians rejected the idea that freedom was an individual thing. An individual could not be truly free if others in his community weren't. Social changes were the key. Without these changes in the practical bits of your life, your religious life could not be improved. Your relationship with God could only get better if you were freed from oppression and given back a sense of your own individual freedom and power. Liberation Theology argues that God has a bias towards the poor. They believed that the poor should be every Christian's first priority.

Christian Revolution?

Liberation Theologians argued that the poor would have to work together to improve their lives. They challenged the ruling classes, and argued that the ruling elites would have to change if they wanted to avoid the poor rising up in possibly violent revolution. Most Liberation Theologians opposed the use of violence. The Church's leaders worried that Liberation Theology might;

◆ Lead to violent revolution

◆ Lead people away from Christianity to Marxism, and so eventually atheism

◆ Lead to the ruling classes going against Christianity – which could have its own problems.

For these reasons, the Church kept the Liberation theologians at arm's length. Some even "accused" them of abandoning Christianity and turning to Marxism, showing that they thought these are opposites. Liberation Theologians questioned the Church's attitude to the poor. This wasn't always welcomed, so Liberation Theologians didn't have an easy time of it. But what did they do?

Gustavo Gutierrez (1928–)

In 1971 he wrote the first major Liberation Theology work, *The Theology of Liberation*. Like many Liberation Theologians he was a priest who went to live with the poor, in his case in the slums of Lima, Peru. It is out of his daily work with the poor, living as one of them, that his beliefs have evolved. This is a common feature of Liberation Theologians. They don't write their ideas hidden away in libraries or at computers using books – their teachings come out of their direct experience of living life in poverty. For Gutierrez, individual salvation comes with liberation from economic and social oppression. Gutierrez says;

> **Task**
> Discuss: Can you only understand poverty once you have been poor yourself?

> **Task**
> Discuss: Who do you think might oppose Liberation Theologians? Why? Do you think some might see them as threatening? Why might a Christian be worried by their "Marxist" views?

Liberation Theology was born in the midst of Latin America's poverty. This poverty still exists. When poverty disappears, Liberation Theology will no be needed any more. I will be very happy if that happens!

www.neue-lz.ch

Gutierrez argued that you couldn't understand poverty unless you lived with it. Gutierrez makes it quite clear that he shares life with the poor in order to take it on. It's evil, and he protests against it by living with it when he doesn't have to. Gutierrez calls this *showing solidarity* with the poor. This might bring poverty to the attention of those in power and force them to think about it more carefully.

Oscar Romero, martyr for the poor

On 24 March 1980, Archbishop Oscar Romero was assassinated as he was saying mass. Romero was initially unimpressed with the whole idea of Liberation Theology. He thought it was too political and too likely to lead people away from the faith. But in San Salvador, where he was Archbishop, the government treated its opponents brutally. Death squads, organised by the government, went around the country torturing and killing opponents. A number of Romero's priests were killed because of their speaking out for the poor. In San Salvador itself, the death squads killed hundreds of people every week. Sometimes their bodies were left hanging from trees in the streets.

Romero stuck to peaceful means of protest. He argued that the "battle" between Communism and Capitalism was a "world war" being fought out on the streets of his own city. He wasn't all that interested in the differences between Communist philosophy and Christian teaching – he was simply on the side of the poor. So he was very much in the tradition of *praxis* – or practical action in favour of the poor. He remained loyal to the traditions and leaders of the Church while still working tirelessly for the poor with whom he lived.

Oscar Romero

BELIEF AND ACTION

Dom Helder Camara

A survivor of assassination attempts, Camara is another well-known Liberation Theologian. Like many Liberation Theologians, he argued that doing nothing to oppose oppression is just as bad as causing it. He believed that political philosophy wasn't the answer. Direct action to help the poor and to make people aware of their conditions was what was necessary. He too supported the "preferential option for the poor". Like others, his beliefs developed through his working with and living beside the poor and oppressed.

Should Christians get involved in politics?

Some think that Christians should stick to prayer and worship. Others say that politics is about every aspect of your life. So too, is Christianity. Christians therefore have a responsibility to speak out against things which are wrong. Jesus challenged both the religious and the political leaders of his day. He didn't suggest that the people should rise up in revolution, but that they should all change their ways so that they lived good lives and returned to God. Jesus showed compassion to his own people but also to the rulers. He even healed the servant of an enemy soldier. He also said that people should "Give to Caesar what is his, and to God what is his". Jesus could probably have roused the people to revolution if he'd wanted to, but this obviously wasn't his way. He seemed to see a need for some to rule and some to be ruled, but wanted this to be done with love, care and compassion. His argument was that the difference was not between the powerful and the powerless, but between those who lived in God and those who didn't. In his meeting with the governor Pontius Pilate, he stated quite clearly that all power comes from God. Meaning that if your life is centred on God, then your use of power will be just and fair.

Capitalists and Proletariat are all God's children

Many Christians are uncomfortable with the idea of the option for the poor. They think that God has no bias towards anyone. Marx believed that the ruling elite should be overthrown. But Christians must also show love to the ruling elite too. This doesn't mean you ignore the wrong they do. It does mean that you show Christian love to all – rich and poor, powerful and powerless, oppressors and oppressed You can hate the sin but love the sinner.

> **Task**
>
> Imagine you had to interview these three Liberation Theologians. What questions might you ask them?

> **Task**
>
> Do you think a Christian should get involved in politics? Explain your views.

Jesus' teaching about wealth and poverty has many faces. On the one hand he seems to accept private ownership of property, but on the other hand he sends the rich young ruler away unhappy, fearing that he'll never get into heaven. Jesus does stress love for all though – this would definitely put the brakes on the possibility of violent revolution. Marx seemed to say that the oppressed must take control of their situation and boot out those who are causing them problems. Jesus doesn't say that the poor should just accept their lot, but he teaches that where people have the right relationship with God, there won't be any oppressed, and so there won't be a need for any revolution.

For some Christians, this is the key issue as far as Liberation Theology is concerned. The poor have to take charge for themselves. Others argue that this will just lead to social unrest – possibly more violence. The point is to change the hearts of the rich and powerful, so they use their positions wisely. But how long should the poor wait? Which is the best way to change the world – Christianity or Marxism?

Task

Do you think Christianity or Marxism is the best way to help the poor and oppressed? Explain your answer.

Source A

www.osjspm.org

As followers of Christ, we are challenged to make a fundamental "option for the poor" – to speak for the voiceless, to defend the defenceless, to assess life styles, policies and social institutions in terms of their impact on the poor. This "option for the poor" does not mean pitting one group against another but rather, strengthening the whole community by assisting those who are the most vulnerable. As Christians, we are called to respond to the needs of all our brothers and sisters, but those with the greatest needs require the greatest response

Economic Justice for all (pastoral message no. 16)

Comments

This comes from a website which cites Catholic Social teaching on the theme of the option for the poor. It clearly shows that many Catholics believe that the needs of the poor should come first, but that fixing these needs doesn't need to result in violence, or even in social unrest. Many Christians believe that the needs of the poor can be sorted out without the kind of revolution which Marx proposed.

Source B

The deepest reason for voluntary poverty is love of neghbour. Christian poverty has meaning only as a commitment of solidarity with the poor, with those who suffer misery and injustice. The commitment is to witness to the evil which has resulted from sin and is a breach of communion. It is not a question of idealising poverty, but rather of taking it on as an evil to protest against it and to struggle to abolish it. Because of this solidarity . . . one can also help the poor and exploited to become aware of their exploitation and seek liberation from it. Christian poverty, and expression of love, is solidarity with the poor and is a protest against poverty . . . it is lived . . . as an authentic imitation of Christ . . .

Gustavo Gutierrez *A Theology of Liberation,* (Orbis, Maryknoll, NY 1988)

Comments

Gutierrez responds to those who have argued that living with the poor is some kind of stunt. He argues that for someone to give up links with their own class and social group and to go and live with the poor is a way of protesting against the privileges of your own social group. Making people aware of the problems of poverty is one step along the road of getting rid of it.

◆ Oscar Romeros' entrails, removed before his body was embalmed, are still miraculously intact

◆ In Latin America today, 25% of people live below the poverty line

◆ In El Salvador, 40 in every 1000 children die before they're 5. In Britain, the figure is 7 in every 1000

Facts and Figures

Activities

Knowledge and Understanding

Intermediate 1

1 Choose the right answers for this quiz from the list below;
   a Of the 4.4 billion people in developing countries, this fraction have no adequate housing.
   b This fraction lacks basic sanitation.
   c Poverty isn't just lack of material wealth, it's this too . . .
   d Christians believe God made the world like this.
   e This is where developing world countries owe money.
   f This kind of government often sides with the rich and powerful.

   Corrupt   Three fifths   One quarter Having no choices in life   Debt With plenty for all to share

2 Give one reason why a Marxist might not like a Christian.

3 Some think the Christian Church is on the side of the rich and powerful. If that's true, which of the following statements could support this view?
   a Christians believe that governments are chosen by God.
   b Many Christians have died for opposing unjust rulers.
   c The Church has opposed unfair rulers.

4 Copy and complete this quote, putting the underlined words in the right order.

When I <u>Communist</u> the <u>saint</u> they called me a <u>poor</u>. When I <u>poor</u>, "<u>Why</u> are they <u>asked</u>?" they called me a <u>fed</u>"

5 What made the first Liberation Theologians start asking questions about the poor?

6 In your own words, what three things does Liberation Theology mean?

7 What does it mean to say that God has a bias towards the poor? What do you think?

8 Why did the Church worry about the teachings of the Liberation Theologians?

9 How did Gustavo Gutierrez develop his ideas?

10 Why was Oscar Romero assassinated?

11 Why did Dom Helder Camara criticise both the USA and the USSR?

12 Draw up two columns.

   Arguments for Christians taking part in Politics
   Arguments against Christians taking part in Politics

   Put these comments into the correct column:
   a Politics is about every aspect of your life
   b Christians should only worry about getting it right with God

Activities continued

c Jesus challenged the politicians in his day

d Jesus healed the Roman Soldier's servant

e Jesus said all power comes from God

13 Should a Christian treat Capitalists the same way a Marxist would? Explain your answer.

14 Read Source A again. What does "Option for the Poor" mean?

15 Read Source B again. Why did Gutierrez live with the poor?

Intermediate 2

1 According to CAFOD, what are the major features of poverty?

2 What does it mean to say that poverty is more than the lack of material wealth? Do you aree?

3 Are people any less oppressed today than they were in Marx's day?

4 Why might a government go against its own people?

5 Why do you think Christians and Marxists have not always worked together to help the poor and oppressed?

6 Why might Christians support the ruling classes?

7 What do the Liberation Theologians mean by *praxis*?

8 What do the Liberation Theologians mean by the "option for the poor"?

9 What would be the likely Christian response to the idea of revolution?

10 Why might some Christians feel that Liberation Theology could be a dangerous way for Christians to try to help the poor?

11 How would Gutierrez respond to the criticism that Liberation Theology was just a gimmick?

12 How did Oscar Romero come to change his beliefs about the way for a Christian to help the poor?

13 Why might Camara have argued that doing nothing was just as bad as doing something?

14 Outline the arguments for and against a Christian getting involved in politics.

15 In your opinion, what would Jesus think of Marxism?

16 Read Source A again. Does this quote support or reject Marxist revolution?

17 Read Source B again. How does Gutierrez defend his life with the poor?

Practical Activities

1 Do some further research into the three Liberation Theologians in this section. Design an information leaflet about their life, teachings and work.

2 Do some further research into the countries in which they operated. Brazil, Peru and El Salvador. Write a magazine article afterwards entitled: "The poor in Latin America in the 21st century – what's changed?"

3 The Roman Catholic Church is currently looking into whether or not Oscar Romero should be made a saint. Write a letter to the Pope outlining whether you think Romero should be made a saint or not.

4 Find out which people involved in politics come from Christian backgrounds. How does their Christianity help them. Famously, Tony Blair is a Christian. Perhaps you could write to him and ask him about what he's doing as a Christian Prime Minister to help the poor.

Practical Activities continued

5 It is very difficult to imagine poverty unless you experience it. Think about how much you spend on yourself every week. Now reduce this amount by 94%. See how you manage through the week, and write a short report about your experience. How did doing with less make you feel?

6 Imagine you're a Christian. Your church has links with a group of Christians in Latin America. They are being pushed into taking part in a Marxist style revolution. What advice might you give them? Write a letter to them outlining your views.

Unit Assessment Question

Intermediate 1: Outcome 1:
What is meant by Liberation Theology?

Intermediate 2: Outcome 2:
How should a Christian respond to Marx's teachings about revolution as the best way to help the oppressed?

Sample Exam Question

Intermediate 1:
"Marxism does little for the oppressed." Do you agree? Give two reasons for your answer. (4)

Intermediate 2:
To what extent should a Christian support revolution? (6)

Homework

Find out about the work of CAFOD. What does it do to help the poor and oppressed in the world today?

Funtime

Howard, a rich Christian from Edinburgh goes to bed one night as usual (thanking God for all the nice things that have happened to him that day). When he wakes up he's a little surprised. This is due to him having woken up in a room with a corrugated tin roof in a slum in Latin America. As you can imagine, everyone's a little surprised at this turn of events. Eduardo is also a Christian, and it's his "house" Howard's woken up in. After a brief discussion along the lines of "Where did you come from . . . ?" Eduardo begins to ask some awkward questions about what Howard's been doing in Edinburgh to help Eduardo and his fellow Christians. Write, or act out, the discussion they might have.

Revision and Study Guide

What this course has been about

By now you should be an expert of sorts in RMPS. You should know a great deal more about the topics you have studied.

These days, you can get all the information you want – and plenty you don't from the Internet. But sometimes it's hard to wade through all the pigpoo to find the diamonds inside. Lots of my pupils tell me that they can't really be bothered with the Internet, because they waste so much time actually trying to find something useful – and anyway, they don't always spot what's useful when they see it. Hopefully this book is a bit like some babyfood for your brain – it's partially digested and worked out for you so it's easier for you to take in.

You should also now be better at analysing the information you have. RMPS is full of different viewpoints and beliefs. The topics we look at aren't clean and precise like Maths – they're messy and untidy – just like life. One aim of studying RMPS is to try to tidy this mess up just a little. This involves analysis. All this means is picking things apart to see what they're made up of and then putting them back together again. In RMPS, we do this with arguments, opinions and viewpoints. We match sources up with the beliefs they're claimed to support – we match actions up with the beliefs they're supposed to be based on. We put things to the test. Finally, we evaluate. This simply means weighing things up one against the other. This helps us work out what's true and what isn't true.

Why this matters

Re-read the Introductory section – beliefs are very powerful! They shape people's lives today. They have played their part in making the world the way it is today. They will play their part in deciding what our future might be. Some of the topics in your course might be things you never have to think about again, but that's not the point. As you've been studying these topics you've been developing vital skills in the handling of beliefs. This means that when you're faced with new ideas or claims – you'll be much better at working with them.

Learning Outcomes

The structure of your course should have helped you do all this. You now have a toolkit of sorts with which to cope with the challenges of belief.

◆ **Learning Outcome 1:** This should show that you can demonstrate **knowledge** and **understanding** of issues of belief. What counts as an issue? What challenges does it present for religious belief?

◆ **Learning Outcome 2**: This should show that you can **analyse** issues of belief. So, if you are faced with a particular issue, you can identify and explain the challenge it presents for religious belief. It also means that you can out yourself "in the shoes" of a religious person by explaining what they might say in response to this challenge. This ability to see things from another person's point of view is one of the major skills to be developed in RMPS (and life!).

◆ **Learning Outcome 3**: This should show that you can **evaluate** issues of belief. You should be able to explain and discuss at least two sides of any given issue, but you should also be prepared to use these viewpoints to come to your own reasoned conclusion about the issue. You should be able to support this conclusion with at least two reasons.

(At Intermediate 1 all you're required to do is be able to present one clear personal opinion on an issue of belief supported by at least two appropriate reasons.)

One big benefit of the Nature of Belief Unit is that it is differentiated by outcome. This is fancy teacher-talk for saying that you cover the same topics at Intermediate 1 and Intermediate 2 – and then show what level you're at by the depth and breadth with which you're able to cope with the topics and issues. This means also that the learning outcomes are more or less the same at both levels – though you'll find the phrasing of questions is a little more complex at Intermediate 2 level.

How do Teachers and Markers know what level you are?

Some subjects are easy to judge – you get it right or you don't. RMPS isn't one of these. RMPS teachers and markers use things

called Grade Descriptions. This is just a technical way of saying what a C is and what an A is. They apply these Grade Descriptions to your work.

Here are some examples -

Knowledge and Understanding

Grade C = You can show in *some detail* knowledge and understanding of key concepts and issues.
Grade A = You can demonstrate *detailed* knowledge and understanding of key concepts and issues.

In other words, the more detail you put in your answer, the more chance you have of getting an A.

Analysis

Grade C = Distinguish between different interpretations and viewpoints in relation to concepts and issues.
Grade A = Distinguish *in a detailed way* between different interpretations and viewpoint in relation to concepts and issues.

In other words, the more detail you put into your analysis of the issues, the more chance you have of getting an A.

Evaluation

Grade C = Present a clear personal conclusion *supported by two appropriate reasons.*
Grade A = Present a clear personal conclusion with some *supporting argument.*

In other words, the more detail there is in your supporting argument, the more chance you have of getting an A.

Assessment

There are two major ways you're formally assessed. The first is the Unit Assessment, and the second is the Exam. A Unit Assessment (your teacher might call it a NAB) is an end of unit test. The same questions are used all over the country to make sure everyone has the same chance. This is marked by your teacher. S/he then tells you and the SQA whether you've passed or not – sometimes the SQA sends people to your school to check your teacher's marking of these NABs. The Exam is marked by markers appointed by the SQA – who are just RMPS teachers from other schools by the way.

What follows is a sample NAB answer for the three Learning Outcomes.

Different topic material has been used to give some variety in the answers. It's up to your teacher to make sure that you understand what a real NAB will be made up of.

Intermediate 1

IA1 Why might the Big Bang Theory be a challenge for religious people?

Good – states what the Big Bang theory is

The Big Bang Theory says that everything in the universe began at one moment – everything including space and time itself. Some religious people like it because it looks as if it needed something to start it off – could it be God? But other religious people don't like it because if there wasn't a before the Big Bang – where and when could there have been a God?

Good variety of religious responses to the challenge

Scientists say that the Big Bang didn't need to be set off by anyone or anything. It could just have been physics equations. Again, this means there's no place for God – unless he's just the laws of physics. Religious people like to think there's a point to everything. If the Big Bang is true, then this is a problem for religious people because the Big Bang was just a pointless, lucky event. **(138)**

Good indication that religious response is concerned with meaning

Scientific challenge clearly identified

IA2 Marx said that God is just an imaginary figure used to keep people in their place. How might a Christian respond to this?

Clear statement of Marx's position

Marx thought that religion was used as a "social tool" by the ruling classes to keep people down. This was so the proletariat – ordinary people like you and me – could be exploited by the Capitalists. He said that believing in God meant you'd just put up with this rotten treatment, because you'd hope to get your reward in heaven after you die.

Good "technical terminology"

Good use of example

But this is a really negative way of looking at religion. This did happen in Marx's day, but it doesn't prove that God's a fake. Many people's lives have been turned around by believing in God. Like Cammy Mackenzie who was violent and is now a Minister helping people. If God wasn't real, then amazing changes like this wouldn't happen to people. So Marx is wrong, God is real. People who've been converted prove it. **(138)**

Clear rejection of Marxist view

Good – outlines Christian response

Strong conclusion

IA3 "The Universe is perfect, so God must have made it"
Do you agree? Give two reasons for your answer

This is the Argument from Design. St Thomas Aquinas came up with this one. He said that everything in the universe seemed just right for its purpose, so there must have been something to make it that way. Only something like God could do such a thing. So – God must exist.

Clear opening – referring clearly to Aquinas

Good analysis and reflection of Aquinas

I agree with Aquinas that the universe is very well-ordered. Everything does seem to fit in really well. So it could look as if it had been made. But I'm not so sure. It could all just have come about by chance over millions of years and just looks ordered. This doesn't have to mean that anything's behind it – it could just be the laws of nature. If it was God, how do you explain the things which don't work so well? Did God make some mistakes along the way? It's a bit much to say that the universe is perfect!

Good first point

Reason 1

Well developed now with supporting argument

Also, even if we could prove that something did make it all, that doesn't mean it was God as we know him. It could have been a committee of Gods, or a different God completely. So no, I don't agree with the statement. **(195)**

Reason 2

Second point well made

Intermediate 2

IA1 Humanists claim that religious experiences can't be used as proof that God exists. How might a religious person respond to this claim?

A Christian would want to argue that a religious experience points towards there being a God. To say that it's just in your head is a clear challenge to religious belief. Many Christians have been changed by religious experiences – almost always for the better. Some Christians would argue that this is the good thing about Christianity – "God finds you". If God is all-powerful, as Christians claim he is – causing someone to experience him isn't going to be all that difficult. Maybe sometimes God thinks it is a good idea to give someone an experience like this as a boost to their faith or even to get their faith off the ground. A Humanist would just look for some other explanation for the experience. Perhaps the person has a very vivid imagination, maybe their mind is being influenced by drugs or alcohol – or maybe the person's emotions have been whipped up into a religious frenzy by some way out church service. Whatever the real explanation was, it couldn't be God because Humanists don't believe in God. There's the problem – Humanists start out not believing in God and so obviously they won't think religious experiences are possible. This isn't a very scientific approach (and Humanists like the scientific approach), because they're just starting off with one belief rather than another.

A religious person would also say that religious experiences can be nice and quiet and not very dramatic – but then God has his ways. Christians would say that Humanists can't prove that religious experiences are false any more than Christians can prove they point to God.
(264)

Good statement of the challenge

Argument 1

Argument 2

Good development of argument

Counter arguments are well set out

Developed criticism of Humanist viewpoint

Good conclusion – reflecting the inconclusive nature of the debate

IA2: "Science and Religion *both* adequately explain the origin of the universe". How far might a religious person agree?

Good clear reference to source

They could easily agree with this statement. The idea of non-overlapping magisteria as stated by SJ Gould explains this view. Gould says that religion and science should stick to their own areas of understanding. It's only when they try to answer each other's questions that the sparks fly. Science explains the origin of the universe by the Big Bang Theory. This says that space, time and matter all began in an instant – for reasons not yet understood.

Development in use of source

Good explanation of scientific position

Good development of what Big Bang theory might mean for some Christians

Some religious people have jumped on the fact that what caused the Big Bang isn't understood by science. But this will just lead to the "God of the Gaps" theory. If science does explain what caused the Big Bang, then religious people will have to think again if they'd said it was God. The Big Bang theory can be proved by the background radiation in the universe today, the amount of materials around and everything in the universe is moving apart as if there had been a Big explosion. God cannot be proved in this scientific way. But then, that's the point – God can't be proved by science because there's no scientific way to do that. God has to be "proved" in a different way.

Good reference

Evidence in support of Big Bang is clearly stated

Religious people explain that God made the universe. This is written in their holy books like the Bible in Genesis, "God made the earth and he saw that it was good". But the Bible isn't meant to be a science book explaining how God did it, it's just a way of showing that God did do it – and so there's a point to it. The Bible is just a babytalk way of explaining – who'd understand if God said how he really did it? Religious people don't try to answer science questions using the Bible – so scientists shouldn't try to answer religious questions using test-tubes.

Good use of source

Well-developed argument from the religious perspective

Good – conclusion draws previous elements of the answer together

So, in conclusion, science could be right in saying that the universe began with a Big Bang, but it can't tell us why this happened when it didn't need to, or what that means for our life. Religion can tell us this. So both explanations can be right. **(355)**

IA3: To what extent do you agree that Christians can support Marxist revolution?

Good – identifies Marx's 'confusion' right away

This is not an easy question, because we don't really know what kind of revolution Marx thought was right. He did believe in revolution. He thought that the ruling classes had to be overthrown by the proletariat if the oppressed were to get justice in their lives and stop being exploited by capitalists. He said "workers of the world unite, you have nothing to lose but your chains". If he meant people taking control of their own lives then a Christian could agree with this. Christians believe that everyone deserves a chance in life, and that all should be treated equally. One group shouldn't oppress another. The Bible says that "all are one in Christ Jesus" – so this means that people shouldn't be exploited and oppressed just because they were born in a low social class. The Bible is very strong on justice. Christians believe that the Kingdom of God means bringing justice to everyone. If this is done by some kind of revolution then that's OK.

Good explanation of Marx's position

Use of source is good

Good analysis of possible Christian response

Good use of source in context

Developed argument

Liberation Theologians like Gustavo Gutierrez don't think the Church has done enough to help the oppressed. Living with the poor has made him realise this. He believes that the oppressed should take control of their own lives and work against the government if it's unfair (even though many Christians think you should support the government because God chose it). Sometimes the Church has been annoyed by these Liberation Theologians, because it worries that they'll turn people away from Christianity and towards Marxism (Marx was an atheist after all!).

Handles the challenge of Liberation Theology well

Good development of responses within Christianity to Liberation Theology

The major problem for Christians is the use of violence. Sometimes Marx seemed to say that violent revolution was the only way. Communist revolutionaries like Che Geuvara used violence to overthrow rulers. Christians would generally not support the use of violence, because this goes against the teachings of Jesus. So, if Marxist revolution meant violent revolution, then most Christians would not support it. **(318)**

Use of example

Focuses well on the key elements of the issue

Good unambiguous conclusion

The Exam

In your exam, you'll have to answer questions on Units you have studied.

By the time you get to the exam you'll know a great deal about the topics and you'll have thought through your views carefully.

The exam isn't meant to trick you, it's a chance for you to show what you can do, not what you can't. Here are a few tips.

◆ **The Marker wants you to do well**: Some of us are quite slushy really. We know that an exam can be scary, and we want you to do well. So, we try as hard as we can to make sure that we give you credit for your answer. We're teachers, just like your own teachers, and we got into the job because we want to make the world a better place! The more people learn in RMPS, and the more people who pass the exam, the happier we'll be!

◆ **Answer the question fully**: Stick to the point and weigh things up. Don't write ten times as much for a question which is worth four marks than for one which is worth ten marks. Remember to answer the question set – don't just write all you know about...

◆ **Explain things**: Sometimes candidates just state something and expect the marker to "know what I mean". Make sure that what you've written quite clearly lets the marker know what you mean.

◆ **Give your answers a clear structure**: A beginning, middle and end is a good starting point. Otherwise you'll lose the thread of what you're saying, forget things, lose the plot generally. This helps stop you going off into la la land.

◆ **Back up your ideas wherever possible**: Use sources as much as you can – if you can quote it perfectly in the right place then that's perfect – but even if you only give a nod in the right direction of a source – for example, "in the Bible it says that you should...", or "Marx himself said...". Many of the questions in this section could be answered without having done a course in RMPS based on your own vague ideas. Make sure that you show that you've studied the course by using the source!

◆ **Follow the "rules" of the question**: If a question asks for a conclusion give one, if it asks whether you agree or not – say so. If it asks you to compare views, do it. Your answer should reflect what the question asks, not what you want it to ask.

◆ **Re-read your answers**: You'll remember other things to add or make things more clear by fiddling about with what you've already written. You might notice terrible mistakes or mind-boggling confusion. You'll have a chance to fix it, but not if you don't re-read it.

This course and this book has been designed to get you thinking about some very important questions in life, and to work out what they mean for you. Don't just forget about it all after your exam. Thinking about beliefs is something which you'll do for the rest of your life. The skills you've developed here will hopefully help you throughout your life in all sorts of ways. Beliefs matter.
Thank you for thinking it through.

Joe Walker
mobyjoe1uk@yahoo.co.uk

Index

Index

Index